The Sweet Bread Machine Cookbook

Melissa Clark

D1560203

B

BERKLEY BOOKS, NEW YORK

THE SWEET BREAD MACHINE COOKBOOK

A Berkley Book / published by arrangement with
the author

PRINTING HISTORY
Berkley edition / March 1997

The Putnam Berkley World Wide Web site address is
http://www.berkley.com/berkley

ISBN: 0-425-15695-8

BERKLEY®
Berkley Books are published by The Berkley Publishing Group,
200 Madison Avenue, New York, New York 10016.
BERKLEY and the ''B'' design
are trademarks belonging to Berkley Publishing Corporation.

PRINTED IN THE UNITED STATES OF AMERICA

10 9 8 7 6 5 4 3 2 1

TO MY SISTER AMY CLARK

Acknowledgments

Special thanks to:

The Zojirushi Corporation, for providing me with the means to this end.

Malena Watrous, my industrious intern, who helped test every recipe in this book and then helped me eat or give away all the bread.

Ana Deboo, who gave up a sunny spring afternoon to help with the tedious job of proofreading.

Robin Aronson, who would have given up many sunny afternoons to help, but instead offered constant encouragement.

Josh Mack, because I didn't include him elsewhere.

Lee Ann Chearney, of course, for excellent agenting and everything else.

P.C.&E., for etc.

CONTENTS

Contents   vii

INTRODUCTION

After writing my first bread machine cookbook and testing over 200 recipes in a very short time span (six weeks, to be exact), when I finally typed that last sentence and gave those sturdy, faithful machines their final wipe-down (I had to keep three going twenty-four hours a day to meet the deadline), I understandably backed away from bread altogether. Shortly after completing that book, I moved. I packed up the remaining bread machine (the others found happy homes in less crowded apartments) and, out of necessity, stowed it in a closet in my new place, which had a kitchen the size of many suburban mudrooms. Sadly, the bread machine never made it out of its box.

When I finally moved into my current, more capacious digs, I unearthed Old Faithful, wiped off the dust, and set the machine to mixing, kneading, and baking the many breads I wrote about in my first bread machine cookbook. I rediscovered and was again delighted by the ease and consistency of the loaves a bread machine afforded, not to mention how delicious they tasted. After a year's hiatus, my bread machine once again took center stage in my kitchen, and I grieved for the calories wasted on inferior bread.

Then I was asked to write a follow-up to the first bread

machine book (cleverly titled *The Bread Machine Cookbook* and still in print), this one focusing on sweet breads. I liked this idea; it legitimized my sweet tooth. Upon consideration, I also realized how perfect the bread machine really is for sweet breads, since it easily delivers a melting, soft-textured loaf through and through. So I began testing. And there were so many brilliant successes (like a buttery, egg-rich brioche that is better than any I had made by hand) that I gained an even greater admiration for my bread machine and broadened my repertoire in the bargain. I now use my machine all the time to make raspberry honey buns for breakfast, orange juice challah for the best French toast ever, or to make multilayered, flaky Danish dough. And, of course, I still make all those wonderful nonsweet loaves I developed in the last go-around.

The next time I move, I will make sure there is enough counter space for my bread machine. And if something must go, the microwave oven will be much less missed, I am sure.

Recipes for some of the ingredients required for these breads can be found elsewhere within the book; or, you may also use a prepackaged version.

INGREDIENTS

YEAST

Yeast is available in two forms: compressed fresh yeast sold in and known as "cakes," and active dry yeast, which is dehydrated yeast granules that become reactivated when mixed with warm water. In a bread machine, you are best off using active dry yeast, since the machines are not programmed for fresh yeast (which reacts a bit faster than the dry). Fresh yeast cakes are also more difficult to find. I usually buy my active dry yeast in bulk at a health food store since it is much less expensive that way. Yeast keeps very well in the refrigerator, although if you are using what you bought from bulk and there is no expiration date, make sure to proof it before adding to the machine. To proof yeast, mix the amount called for with a bit of warm (90–115 degrees F) water and a pinch of sugar and wait ten minutes. It should react and bubble. If not, discard it and buy new yeast.

Flour

In this book, unlike in my last one, I always use all-purpose flour. This is because bread flour contains a stronger gluten network, which is what gives bread its sturdy structure. For sweet breads, a softer, more delicate texture is called for, and so is a flour with a lower gluten content. However, cake flour, which has the lowest gluten content of all wheat flours, is not good for yeast-risen sweet breads, since some gluten is needed to trap the gas given off by the yeast, which in turn causes the dough to rise. Thus, all-purpose flour is a good compromise since it has a medium-amount gluten. You can use either bleached or unbleached flour, although unbleached is always preferable for environmental reasons.

EGGS

Eggs add protein to bread and help to build up the structure and lighten the texture. The yolk imparts a wonderful richness and a deep yellow hue to the crumb, which is essential in many of the recipes in this book. In general, if you are trying to avoid eggs, choose from the many recipes that do not include them, rather than substituting egg whites for whole eggs. These are sweet breads; they are meant to be somewhat decadent. I always use grade A large or extra-large eggs (not that I have ever come into contact with a grade B egg). They are the default for most baking.

LIQUIDS

Some type of liquid is necessary to activate the yeast and bind the loaf. Water, the most basic liquid, is not used in sweet breads as often as it is in other bread since it will produce a crisper crust than is desirable in dessert. Milk will yield a smoother, more tender interior than water and will improve a loaf's keeping qualities. In this book, I tested with whole milk, although in most cases you can substitute skim or low-fat (I specify whole milk when it is absolutely necessary). However, the richer the liquid, the more tender the crumb. Buttermilk and sour cream are also often used in sweet breads and contribute their tangy, rich flavor. Plain yogurt can be substituted for either one, by the way.

Other liquids used in this book include fruit juice, for its flavor, and liquor and liqueurs, also for flavor. However, too much alcohol will kill the yeast, so make sure to measure carefully and follow the directions when adding it to your loaves.

SUGAR AND SWEETENERS

Obviously these are essential, since they are what makes a sweet loaf sweet. I have used all kinds of sweeteners in this book, depending upon the qualities I'm after. Sugar always means granulated white sugar, unless I specify something else such as brown sugar. You can substitute honey for some of the sugar, but make sure to cut back on the other liquids in the recipe, or the dough will be too wet. For sugar-related loaf catastrophes, see the chapter on bread machine tips and troubleshooting under "Soggy Crumb Syndrome."

SHORTENING

Butter is without a doubt my shortening of choice for sweet breads. It produces a rich tasting, delicate loaf with a flaky texture and soft, melting crumb. Personally, I do not believe in margarine or solid vegetable shortening for sweet breads, although technically, substituting either for the butter will not harm the structure of your loaf. But it won't taste nearly as good. I always use unsalted butter, which is usually made with better-quality cream than the salted stuff and is apt to be fresher. When adding butter to the bread machine, follow the directions for either cutting it into small pieces (if there is more than two tablespoons in a recipe) or softening it. This helps it amalgamate better.

Sometimes, I use a combination of butter and olive oil; this is because I want the olive flavor, so make sure to use a potent, extra virgin olive oil since you are only going to use a little. You can substitute unflavored oil, such as canola or corn or safflower, for the butter, if you are health savvy.

SALT

Salt is added to bring out the flavor of the loaf and to inhibit the yeast, which tends to go a bit berserk when surrounded by all that sugar. Use sea salt if you can; it tastes better. If you are following a low-sodium diet, you may cut back on the amount of salt in these recipes, but do not leave it out altogether.

BREAD MACHINE TIPS AND TROUBLESHOOTING

In my first bread machine book, I wrote several pages on tips for getting the most out of your bread machine and the ways to correct and compensate for the inevitable snafu. When working with sweet and enriched doughs, the list of potential calamities grows even longer because sugar, butter, and eggs, which are essential ingredients in these loaves, do not always happily coexist with yeast. Too much sugar, and the loaf will sink the middle, since the yeasts gorge on the plenty and render themselves inactive, like many of us after Thanksgiving dinner. Too much fat from egg yolks and butter and, like an athlete trying to lift weights if her muscles are weighted down under sheaths of fat, the gases produced by the yeast are unable to lift the heavy dough to rise. Below are some tips to get around these deterrents that will enable you to make your loaves sweet, rich, and raised all at once.

MACHINE DIFFERENCE

Bread machines differ from brand to brand, and each is chock-full of idiosyncracies. I tested the recipes in this book in a Zojirushi home bakery and found it to be dependable and sturdy, a regular workhorse, but not without quirks. One thing to be aware of is the order in which you place the ingredients into the bread pan. In writing these recipes, I have placed the ingredients in an order beginning with liquids and ending with flour and yeast, because that is the way most machines are made to handle them. If your machine wants the yeast first, by all means acquiesce.

Overall, the most important thing to producing consistently delicious loaves is to get to know your bread machine, from the inside out. In general, it is best to begin following the directions that came with your model and then to adapt them for your own use. As they say, you need to know the rules in order to successfully improvise.

One way to become intimate with your bread machine is to peek under the hatch during the kneading cycle. Are the ingredients coming together into a satiny-smooth bouncing ball of dough? Or does the ball stick to the sides of the machine, feel wet and tacky, and relax into the corners of the pan when the kneading is finished? This might indicate that the dough contains too much liquid. Or it might be the character of the dough you are making. A wet, batterlike dough is not uncommon in sweet breads. However, does your dough clump up, twist around the kneading paddle, and seem uneven during rising? This is almost never desirable, and you may have added too much flour, or the flour you used may be particularly dry (which is common in the winter, when indoor heating sucks all the moisture out of it). If your dough seems too dry to coalesce, add a bit more liquid.

Ultimately, you are in control of your loaves, so peek away and be ready to compensate if necessary.

SETTINGS

If you can, set your bread machine for the shortest baking time and the lightest crust. Many of the newer machines have a setting for sweet breads, and it is a good idea to use them. If you are adding raisinlike embellishments, make sure either to use the raisins setting (and listen for that beep!) or to know when the first kneading cycle is almost over. Then add your chocolate chips or nuts or what have you, so that they don't get pulverized by the kneading paddle, a brutal experience for them.

On the other hand, if you want homogenization, as for adding chocolate pieces that you wish to have melted into the dough or nuts that you want ground up, add them at the beginning with the other ingredients. They will disappear into the dough in no time.

SOGGY CRUMB SYNDROME

The most common failing of baking sweet breads in the bread machine is a damp, soggy interior crumb. The reason for this is usually leaving the bread in the pan too long. As soon as the bread machine cycle is finished, immediately remove the bread pan from the machine (use oven mitts because the pan is hot) and turn the loaf out onto a wire rack to cool. Then, make sure to cool the loaf thoroughly before slicing it, or the pressure from the knife may squish the crumb, making it seem heavy. Another cause of an underbaked appearance could be too much sugar in the loaf, so make sure to only use the amount called for in the recipe.

THE DOORSTOP LOAF

You've followed all the directions, added the correct amount of sugar, but have still ended up with a dense, heavy brick more suitable to masonry than breakfast. Here's the rub: while adding the right amount of butter and/or fat will give your loaf a soft crumb and delicate flavor, too much will prevent it from rising. To combat this, if a loaf calls for a lot of butter, such as in a brioche, I add it after the first rising. This gives the dough a chance to expand and lighten before it is stiffened with butterfat. Another way to compensate is to turn the bread machine off after the kneading cycle and let the dough rise until it is doubled in bulk. With a rich loaf, this could take longer than the set amount of time that most bread machines are programmed for. However, if you follow the instructions, you shouldn't have too much of a problem.

PASTRIES

QUICK CROISSANTS

When trying to develop a recipe for croissants that could be partially made in the bread machine, I had to test what seemed like endless versions of the pastry. After much rolling, turning, and folding, I realized that croissant dough is just puff pastry made with yeast and allowed to rise. Thus, if one can make rapid puff pastry by incorporating all the butter into the dough at once, why not apply that same principal to a yeast-risen croissant dough? It worked beautifully, and while these croissants may not have quite as many layers as the traditional kind (as is the case with rapid puff pastry versus the standard method), they are still wonderful. And easy. I now want to use croissant dough for everything I might use puff pastry for, from tart crusts to wrapping pâté or salmon, to topping chicken pot pie, since I love the yeasty flavor and chewy, melting texture. This dough also freezes well for up to three months.

The method for quick puff pastry on which I based this croissant procedure originally came from *Cook's Illustrated,* a wonderful bimonthly magazine that is a boon for cooks who always want to know why.

Dough
- 1 cup milk
- 1 large egg
- 1 large egg yolk
- ⅓ cup sugar
- 4 tablespoons nonfat dry milk
- ½ teaspoon salt
- 3½ cups all-purpose flour
- 2½ teaspoons yeast
- 1 cup (2 sticks) unsalted butter, cut into 16 pieces and well chilled or frozen

Glaze
- 1 large egg, well beaten

1. Set your bread machine on the dough cycle or equivalent. Place all the dough ingredients except the butter into the bread machine in an order appropriate to your model. After about 6 minutes of kneading (the dough should look smooth), turn off the machine and let the dough rise in the pan for 1 hour.

2. Place the dough and cold butter in the bowl of a food processor fitted with a steel blade. Pulse the mixture until the butter is just distributed, about 10 to 15 times. Do not overprocess; there should be evenly distributed chunks of butter sticking out of the dough.

3. Turn the dough out onto a well-floured surface and shape the dough into a rough rectangle. Place the dough on top of a floured piece of waxed paper measuring at least 12 × 18 inches. Lightly flour the top of the dough and cover with another sheet of waxed paper the same size as the bottom one. Press dough with a rolling pin to flatten it, then roll it out into a 12 × 18-inch rectangle.

4. Peel off the top piece of waxed paper and invert the dough onto a floured surface. Peel off the remaining sheet of waxed paper. Starting with a short side, fold the dough into thirds. It should now measure 4 × 18 inches. Starting with a short side, roll up the dough tightly. Using your hands, press and mold the dough into a square, wrap in plastic, and refrigerate for at least one hour, and up to two days. For longer storage, freeze the dough for up to three months.

5. When ready to bake, grease two baking sheets. On a lightly floured work surface, roll the dough into an 18 × 12–inch rectangle. Cut the dough in half lengthwise to form 2 long strips. Cut each strip into three 6-inch squares. Cut each square into 2 triangles. Working with one triangle at a time, position it with the point away from you. Roll from the long end toward the point, stretching the ends of the dough out as you go. Tuck the point underneath and form a crescent. Place the croissants on the prepared baking sheets, 1 and ½ inches apart. Brush with the glaze and let them rise, uncovered, until they are almost double in bulk, about 1 to 1 to ½ hours.

6. Preheat the oven to 400 degrees F. Bake the croissants until they are golden-brown, for about 15 minutes. Serve them hot, warm, or at room temperature.

Makes 12

PAINS AU CHOCOLAT

Classically, pains au chocolat are made from croissant or brioche dough enveloping a baton of bittersweet chocolate in the center. The dough for the pains is cut precisely the same length as the batons, so that the chocolate peeks through at both unsealed ends of dough. However, batons of bittersweet chocolate are a bit scarce in this country, so I substitute chopped chocolate, which delivers the same flavor, if not the same look.

1 recipe of quick croissant dough (page 12), chilled
6 ounces bittersweet chocolate, coarsely chopped (or use bittersweet chocolate chips)
1 large egg, well beaten, for glazing

1. On a lightly floured surface, roll out the dough into a 12 × 18–inch rectangle. Dust the dough very lightly with flour. Fold the sheet in half lengthwise. Unfold the sheet and cut in half along the crease. You should have two rectangles measuring 6 × 18. Cut each rectangle in half the long way. You will now have four 3 × 18-inch strips. Cut each into four pieces, measuring about 3 × 4 inches.
2. Divide the chocolate into sixteen portions. Place a portion of chocolate in a thin strip lengthwise along one side (about ½ an inch from the edge) of each piece of dough. Starting with the long side closest to the chocolate, loosely roll up the dough to enclose the chocolate.
3. Grease two baking sheets. Place the pains on the sheets, seam side down, leaving 2 inches between each one. Press each pain au chocolat with the heel of your hand to flatten it slightly. Lightly brush the tops with beaten egg, and let them rise until puffy, about 1 to 1 and ½ hours.
4. Preheat the oven to 425 degrees F. Place the pains au chocolat in the oven and reduce the temperature to 400 degrees F. Bake until they are a uniform golden brown and firm to the

touch, 12 to 18 minutes. Slide the pains au chocolat onto a cooling rack. Serve warm or let cool to room temperature and reheat in a 300-degree F oven before serving.

Makes 16

BLACK AND WHITE BRIOCHE BATONS

For this recipe, a cousin to pains au chocolat, I use buttery chocolate brioche instead of flaky croissant dough and white instead of dark chocolate. You can, however, substitute bittersweet or milk chocolate for the white chocolate if you prefer. Some of my favorite combinations include pistachio brioche with dark chocolate, cornmeal with milk chocolate, and brown sugar and candied ginger brioche with white chocolate.

1 recipe chocolate brioche dough (page 65)
4 ounces chopped white chocolate
1 large egg, well beaten, for glazing

1. Roll out the cold dough on a lightly floured work surface to a 12 × 18–inch rectangle about ⅛ inch thick. Scatter the white chocolate pieces or chips over the surface; then press them into the dough with your hand. Fold the short ends of the rectangle toward the middle, so that one short end meets the other in the center.
2. Cut the dough in half along the center seam. Cut each half crosswise in 12 strips, cutting decisively all the way through so that the dough doesn't pull. Place the strips on a greased baking sheet, spacing them about ¾ inch apart. Cover loosely with plastic wrap and let rise until the dough is almost doubled, about 1½ hours.
3. Preheat the oven to 375 degrees F. Lightly brush the tops of the dough strips with the beaten egg. Bake until golden brown, about 15–20 minutes. Cool the batons completely in the pan on a wire rack.

Makes 24

PAINS AUX RAISINS

These pastries were my favorite breakfast, above pains au chocolate and almond croissants even when I was a young girl living in Paris. I would walk with my father, one hand in his and one clutching a floppy string shopping bag, early in the morning to the patissierie and choose the pains aux raisins with the thickest layer of yellow pastry cream escaping the dough. To eat them, it was necessary to break into the outer layer of the spiral and eat the bun in rings, starting with the crisp outside and saving the custardy center for last. I still find myself eating pains aux raisins this way, although not as often as when I was ten.

As always, if you didn't soak your raisins overnight, bring them and the rum to a simmer in a saucepan; then turn off the heat and let them sit for 15 minutes before proceeding with the recipe.

½ **cup raisins soaked overnight in** ¼ **cup dark rum**
1 **recipe chestnut honey brioche dough (page 53)**
1 **recipe pastry cream (page 174)**
3 **tablespoons sugar**
1 **large egg, well beaten, for glazing**
½ **cup confectioners' sugar**

1. Drain the raisins, reserving the rum. On a floured work surface, roll out the brioche dough into a 14-inch square. Trim the sides to make it precise. Spread the pastry cream over the dough with a spatula. Scatter the raisins evenly over the cream; then sprinkle the sugar over the raisins. Starting with a long side, tightly roll up the dough like a jelly roll.
2. Slice the roll into pieces just under 1 inch wide and set them, cut side down, 2 inches apart on a greased baking sheet. Slightly flatten each piece with the palm of your hand; then brush the tops with some of the beaten egg. Let rise, uncovered, for about 1 hour, until the pastries double in bulk.
3. Preheat the oven to 425 degrees F. Brush the pastries with

another coat of beaten egg. Bake until golden brown, about 15 minutes. Remove pan from the oven and transfer pastries with a spatula to cool on a wire rack. Do not shut off the oven.
4. Mix one tablespoon of the reserved rum with the confectioners' sugar and stir into a thin, smooth paste. When the pains aux raisins have cooled, brush the tops with a very thin coating of the sugar mix. Arrange the pastries again on the baking sheet and return them to the oven for 1 to 2 minutes, just until the sugar melts and becomes transparent. Immediately remove pastries from the baking sheet to a wire rack to cool. Serve warm or at room temperature.

Makes 16

LIME RICKEY SPIRALS

Sitting in a lovely garden on an even lovelier spring day, my friend Ana Deboo and I were proofreading the copy for this book (of course, on the day before it was due at the publishers'). When she came upon a recipe I had as a variation for pains aux raisins, using lemon curd instead of pastry cream and dried cherries instead of raisins, she said, "Oh, that's like a lime rickey using lemon instead of lime." It was a brilliant association, and I think the lime is even nicer with cherries than the lemon was.

½ **cup dried cherries**
½ **cup boiling water**
1 **recipe chestnut honey brioche dough (page 53)**
1 **recipe lime curd (page 167)**
3 **tablespoons sugar**
1 **large egg, well beaten, for glazing**

1. Soak the cherries in the boiling water for 15 minutes; then drain them well. On a floured work surface, roll out the brioche dough into a 14-inch square. Trim the sides to make it precise. Spread the curd over the dough with a spatula. Scatter the cherries evenly over the curd, then sprinkle the sugar over the cherries. Starting with a long side, tightly roll up the dough like a jelly roll.
2. Slice the roll into pieces just under 1 inch wide and set them, cut side down, 2 inches apart on a greased baking sheet. Slightly flatten each piece with the palm of your hand; then brush the tops with the beaten egg. Let rise, uncovered, for about 1 hour, until the pastries almost double in bulk.
3. Preheat the oven to 425 degrees F. Bake pastries until they are golden-brown, about 15 minutes. Remove pan from the oven and transfer pastries with a spatula to cool slightly on a wire rack. Serve warm or at room temperature.

Makes 16

SCHNECKEN

Schnecken, which means snails in German, resemble just those. They consist of a sour cream–rich dough rolled up around a raisin, nut, and cinnamon filling, then iced. They are terrific for breakfast or brunch or any time the sweet tooth aches.

This delicate dough must be refrigerated overnight, so plan accordingly.

Dough
    1 cup sour cream
    3 large eggs
    ½ cup (1 stick) unsalted butter, softened
    ¼ cup sugar
    ½ teaspoon salt
    3¼ cups all-purpose flour
    4 teaspoons active dry yeast

Filling
    2 teaspoons ground cinnamon
    ½ cup sugar
    2 tablespoons unsalted butter, melted
    1 cup raisins
    1½ cups chopped toasted walnuts

Glaze
    1 egg white
    1 tablespoon water

Icing
    ½ cup confectioners' sugar
    1½ tablespoons water
    ½ teaspoon pure vanilla extract

1. Set your bread machine on the dough cycle or equivalent. Place all the dough ingredients into the bread machine in an

order appropriate to your model. When the cycle is finished, transfer the dough to a sealed plastic bag and refrigerate it overnight.

2. Preheat the oven to 375 degrees F. Lightly grease a baking sheet. Mix together the cinnamon and sugar. Roll the dough into a 15 × 20–inch rectangle. Brush the top with the melted butter and sprinkle with 3 tablespoons cinnamon sugar; sprinkle on the raisins and chopped nuts. Starting with a long side, roll the dough up jelly roll–style, then cut it into 2-inch pieces.

3. Lay the slices, cut side down, on the prepared baking sheet, spacing them 2 inches apart. Let the pastries rise, uncovered, until doubled in bulk, about 1 hour. Mix the egg white and water together to make a glaze.

4. Brush the pastries with the glaze and sprinkle with the remaining cinnamon sugar. Bake 20 to 25 minutes, until the tops are golden-brown. Remove baking tray to a wire rack to cool slightly.

5. Prepare the icing. In a small bowl, combine the confectioners' sugar, water, and vanilla, mixing until smooth. Using a fork, drizzle the icing over the pastries. Let icing set for at least 20 minutes before serving.

Makes 12

BASIC DANISH DOUGH

This is the basic dough used in the very delicious recipes that follow. It is a bit of a painstaking recipe, but not at all difficult and definitely worth the effort. Danish dough will keep for two days in the refrigerator and up to 3 months frozen.

¾ cups water
2 large eggs, room temperature
2 large egg yolks, room temperature
4 tablespoons (½ stick) unsalted butter, room temperature
¼ cup nonfat dry milk
⅓ cup granulated sugar
1 teaspoon pure vanilla extract
1 teaspoon salt
½ teaspoon ground cardamom, optional
2¾ cups all-purpose flour
1 tablespoon active dry yeast

Filling
1½ cups (3 sticks) unsalted butter, softened
¼ cup all-purpose flour

1. Set your bread machine on the dough cycle or equivalent. Place all the dough ingredients into the bread machine in an order appropriate to your model. After about 5 to 6 minutes into the first kneading cycle (the dough should look smooth), turn the machine off and let the dough rise in the pan for 1 hour. Remove dough from the machine, punch it down, then wrap it in plastic wrap and place in the refrigerator to chill for at least 2 hours.
2. Meanwhile, prepare the filling by combining the butter and flour in the bowl of a food processor or mixer. Process or mix until the flour is incorporated into the butter. Scrape the mixture onto a piece of plastic wrap, form it into a 10 × 14–inch rectangle, and refrigerate it until cold, at least 2 hours.

3. Remove dough from the refrigerator and place on a floured work surface. Roll to a 12 × 20–inch rectangle. If the dough pulls back, allow it to rest for a moment or so before continuing. With the butter mixture still wrapped in plastic, lay the piece on the dough to be certain it covers the lower two-thirds of the dough, with a 1-inch margin of dough projecting around the edges. Unwrap butter and place on dough. Starting with the top third, which is not covered with butter, fold the dough in thirds, as you would a business letter. The butter should be enclosed in the dough.

4. Turn the dough so that one open end is at 6 o'clock and the other at 12 o'clock. Gently roll the layered dough into a 10 × 18 inch rectangle. Sprinkle with flour if butter breaks through.

5. Fold the rectangle of dough into thirds, again like a business letter, and slip into a plastic bag. Refrigerate for 10 minutes.

6. Remove dough from the bag, lay on a floured work surface and roll to a 10 × 18–inch rectangle. Fold into thirds and return to the plastic bag to refrigerate for 20 minutes. Repeat twice more; then return dough to the refrigerator until needed.

DRIED PEACHES AND CHEESE DANISH

Dried peaches have an intensely fruity flavor that leans nicely into the milky cream cheese.

¼ cup chopped dried peaches
¼ cup boiling water, to plump
¾ cup cream cheese
¼ cup sugar
1 tablespoon all-purpose flour
1 large egg
1 teaspoon unsalted butter, melted
2 tablespoons sour cream
½ teaspoon grated lemon zest
½ teaspoon pure vanilla extract
1 recipe basic Danish dough (page 23)

1. In a small bowl, soak dried peaches in boiling water for 15 minutes while assembling other ingredients.
2. In a bowl or food processor, combine the cheese, sugar, and flour, stirring or pulsing to combine. Add the egg, melted butter, sour cream, lemon zest, and vanilla and blend well. Drain the dried peaches and add to mixture. Set aside until needed (filling will last for up to 5 days, refrigerated).
3. Place the chilled dough on a floured work surface and roll it out to a 10 × 15–inch rectangle. Cut the dough into six 5-inch squares. If the squares pull back after cutting, roll each again to the full dimensions.
4. Place a heaping tablespoon of filling in the center of each square and bend two corners inward so that they touch at the center. Place the pastries 1-½-inches apart on a greased baking pan and press the centers down slightly. Cover with plastic wrap and leave to rise for 1 hour.
5. Preheat the oven to 425 degrees F. Bake pastries for 10 minutes before reducing heat to 375 degrees F. Bake until

pastries are golden-brown, about 15 minutes longer. Place pastries on a rack to cool. They may be frozen with excellent results.

Makes 6

MOCHA CUSTARD DANISH PASTRIES

If you really want to gild the lily, add a teaspoon of chocolate chips to each Danish along with the filling.

1 **recipe basic Danish dough (page 23)**
½ **recipe mocha custard filling (page 172)**
  Confectioners' sugar, for sprinkling

1. Place the chilled dough on a floured work surface and roll it out to a 10 × 15–inch rectangle. Cut the dough into six 5-inch squares. If the squares pull back after cutting, roll each again to the full dimensions.
2. Place a heaping tablespoon of filling in the center of each square and bend the four corners inward so that they touch at the center. Place the pastries 1½ inches apart on a greased baking pan and press the centers down slightly. Cover with plastic wrap and leave to rise for 1 hour.
3. Preheat the oven to 425 degrees F. Bake pastries for 10 minutes before reducing heat to 375 degrees F. Bake until pastries are golden-brown, about 15 minutes longer. Place pastries on a rack to cool completely before serving. Sprinkle with confectioners' sugar before serving.

Makes 6

POPPY SEED AND POT CHEESE DANISH

These toothsome Danish pastries remind me of hamantashen (those traditional sweets served during the Jewish festival of Purim) with their triangular shape and poppy seed filling.

½ cup pot, farmers', or ricotta cheese
1 large egg yolk
¼ cup sugar
½ teaspoon pure vanilla extract
½ teaspoon grated lemon zest
½ cup poppy seed filling (page 180)
1 recipe basic Danish dough (page 23)

1. In a bowl or food processor, combine the pot cheese, egg yolk, sugar, vanilla, and lemon zest, stirring or pulsing until smooth. Add the poppy seed filling and mix or pulse until well combined. Set aside until needed (filling will last for up to 5 days, refrigerated).
2. Place the chilled dough on a floured work surface and roll it out ¼-inch thick. Use a 3-inch round cookie cutter to cut circles from the dough. Reroll the scraps and cut out more circles, continuing until all the dough is used.
3. Place a tablespoon of filling in the center of each circle and bend up the sides of the dough to form a triangle; pinch the corners to seal. Place the pastries 1 inch apart on a greased baking pan and cover with plastic wrap. Let pastries rise for 30 minutes.
4. Preheat the oven to 375 degrees F. Bake pastries until they are golden-brown, about 20 minutes. Place pastries on a rack to cool. They may be frozen with excellent results.

Makes 15

RASPBERRY AND ALMOND DANISH SPIRALS

These pastries, full of sweet almond cream and fresh raspberries, are too good only to be made when you have made Danish dough. Feel free to substitute chestnut honey brioche dough, quick croissant dough, or even fresh ginger pastry dough with Kaya (pages 53, 12, 30).

 1 recipe almond cream (page 175)
½ cup fresh raspberries
½ cup sliced blanched almonds
 1 recipe basic Danish dough (page 23)
½ cup confectioners' sugar
 1 tablespoon milk
½ teaspoon almond extract

1. On a floured work surface, roll out the dough into a 14-inch square. Trim the sides to make it precise. Spread the almond cream over the dough with a spatula. Scatter the raspberries and almonds evenly over the cream; then sprinkle the sugar over the filling. Starting with a long side, tightly roll up the dough like a jelly roll.
2. Slice the roll into pieces just under 1 inch wide and set them, cut side down, 2 inches apart on a greased baking sheet. Cover pastries with a damp kitchen towel and let rise for about 1 hour, until almost double in bulk.
3. Preheat the oven to 400 degrees F. Bake pastries until they are golden-brown, about 15 to 18 minutes. Remove pan from the oven and transfer pastries with a spatula to cool slightly on a wire rack.
4. Meanwhile, prepare the icing. In a small bowl, combine the confectioners' sugar, milk, and almond extract, mixing until smooth. Drizzle the icing over the pastries while they are still warm. Let cool completely before serving.

Makes 16

FRESH GINGER PASTRIES WITH KAYA

Fresh and candied ginger give this simplified version of Danish a crisp, spicy flavor, while the kaya (see page 169) adds its perfumed complexity. If you don't want to make kaya, substitute lemon curd, or make the cranberry version below.

The dough must be refrigerated overnight (or for at least 8 hours and up to two days), so plan accordingly.

1 cup sour cream
4 tablespoons (½ stick) unsalted butter, cut into pieces
2 large eggs
3 tablespoons sugar
1 tablespoon fresh grated ginger
1 teaspoon salt
¼ teaspoon baking powder
3 cups all-purpose flour
2½ teaspoons active dry yeast
2 tablespoons candied ginger
1 recipe kaya (page 169)

1. Set your bread machine on the dough cycle or equivalent. Place all the dough ingredients into the bread machine in an order appropriate to your model. When the cycle is finished, transfer the dough to a plastic bag and refrigerate it overnight.
2. The next day, place the chilled dough on a floured work surface and roll it out to a 9 × 15–inch rectangle. Cut the dough into fifteen 3-inch squares. If the squares pull back after cutting, roll each again to the full dimensions.
3. Place a heaping teaspoon of kaya in the center of each square and bend the four corners inward so that they touch at the center. Place the pastries 1 to ½-inches apart on a greased baking pan and press the centers down slightly. Cover with plastic wrap and leave to rise for 40 minutes.
4. Preheat the oven to 425 degrees F. Bake pastries for 10 minutes before reducing heat to 375 degrees F. Bake until

pastries have unfolded somewhat and are golden-brown, about 15 minutes longer. Place pastries on a rack to cool. They may be frozen with excellent results.

Makes 15

ICED FRESH GINGER PASTRIES WITH CRANBERRY CURD

The pink icing on these pastries may be off-putting to those reminded of the florescent frostings of childhood, but the cranberry flavor really makes up for any negative associations.

1 recipe fresh ginger dough (page 30)
1 recipe cranberry curd (page 168)
½ cup confectioners' sugar
1 tablespoon unsweetened cranberry concentrate

1. Set your bread machine on the dough cycle or equivalent. Place all the dough ingredients into the bread machine in an order appropriate to your model. When the cycle is finished, transfer the dough to a plastic bag and refrigerate it overnight.
2. The next day, place the chilled dough on a floured work surface and roll it out to a 9 × 15–inch rectangle. Cut the dough into fifteen 3-inch squares. If the squares pull back after cutting, roll each again to the full dimensions.
3. Place a heaping teaspoon of curd in the center of each square and bend the four corners inward so that they touch at the center. Place the pastries 1½-inches apart on a greased baking pan and press the centers down slightly. Cover with plastic wrap and leave to rise for 40 minutes.
4. Preheat the oven to 425 degrees F. Bake pastries for 10 minutes before reducing heat to 375 degrees F. Bake until pastries have unfolded somewhat and are golden-brown, about 15 minutes longer. Place pastries on a rack to cool.
5. While the Danish are frozen, make the icing. In a small bowl mix the confectioners' sugar and cranberry concentrate together until smooth. Drizzle the icing over the cooled pastries.

Makes 15

HALVAH TWISTS

Halvah becomes rich and caramelized when baked into these flaky twists. Use any kind of halvah you like: pistachio, chocolate marble, almond, or plain.

Dough

¾ cup sour cream
3 tablespoons unsalted butter
2 tablespoons tahini (sesame paste)
¼ cup water
1 large egg
1 large egg yolk, reserving the white for the egg glaze
¼ cup sugar
1 teaspoon salt
¼ teaspoon baking powder
2 tablespoons sesame seeds
3 cups all-purpose flour
2½ teaspoons active dry yeast

Topping

½ cup halvah, crumbled or finely chopped (or frozen, then grated)
½ cup packed dark brown sugar
2 large egg whites
2 tablespoons water
3 tablespoons unsalted butter, melted

1. Set your bread machine on the dough cycle or equivalent. Place all the dough ingredients into the bread machine in an order appropriate to your model. At the end of the final cycle, transfer the dough to a plastic bag and refrigerate it overnight.
2. Grease two baking sheets. Mix the halvah and sugar together in a small bowl and set aside. Stir together the egg whites and water and set aside as well. On a lightly floured board, roll the cold dough out into a 12 × 18–inch rectangle. Cut the dough in half the long way, so that you have two

6 × 18–inch rectangles. Brush the melted butter over both pieces. Sprinkle two-thirds of the halvah mixture over the lower half of each rectangle, reserving the other third for a topping. Use a long metal spatula to flip the top half of the dough over the sugared bottom half and use your palms or a rolling pin to press the dough into the halvah filling.

3. Cut each dough rectangle crosswise into 3-inch strips. You will end up with 18 strips. Carefully pick up each strip with two fingers at each end, twist it in the center, and then place it on a prepared baking sheet. Some of the filling will fall out; that's okay. Allow 2 inches between each twist. Flatten the twists gently with your fingers. Brush them with the egg glaze and sprinkle them with the remaining halvah mixture.

4. Let the twists rise, uncovered, in a warm place for 30 minutes. Preheat the oven to 375 degrees F. Bake the twists for 15 to 20 minutes, or until lightly golden-brown.

Makes 18

TANGERINE AND WALNUT CRESCENTS

These pastries are like rich, yeast-risen rugelach with a tart citrus and nut filling. They are good for breakfast or tea.

½ cup sour cream
¼ cup milk
2 large eggs
6 tablespoons unsalted butter
⅓ cup sugar
¾ teaspoon finely grated orange zest
1 teaspoon salt
3 cups all-purpose flour
1 tablespoon active dry yeast

Filling
Zest of two tangerines (use a vegetable peeler or zester to remove it from the fruit)
½ cup sugar
½ cup toasted walnuts
1 teaspoon pure vanilla extract
2 tablespoons unsalted butter, melted

Glaze
1½ cup confectioners' sugar
3 tablespoons fresh tangerine juice

1. Set your bread machine on the dough cycle or equivalent. Place all the dough ingredients into the bread machine in an order appropriate to your model.
2. Meanwhile, prepare the filling. In a food processor fitted with a steel blade, process the zest, sugar, walnuts, and vanilla until a paste forms. (Filling will last for up to 5 days, refrigerated).
3. When the dough is ready, divide it in half and let rest for 10 minutes. On a lightly floured surface, roll each dough half into a 12-inch circle and spread each with 1 tablespoon of

melted butter. Then spread the filling over the circles. Using a pastry wheel or knife, cut each circle into 12 wedges. Roll up each wedge starting from the wide end; then curve the ends to form a crescent shape. Place the crescents 1½ inches apart on the prepared baking sheets, cover with a kitchen towel, and let rise for 1½ hours, or until doubled in bulk.

4. Preheat the oven to 350 degrees F and bake the crescents for 20 minutes, or until golden.

5. Meanwhile, make the glaze. Mix together confectioners' sugar and tangerine juice until smooth enough to drizzle over the crescents. Glaze the crescents while they're warm. Serve warm or at room temperature.

Makes 24

DRIED AND FRESH CRANBERRY-NUT TURNOVERS

These are holiday-ish. Take advantage.

Dough

  2 large eggs
½ cup sour cream
  4 tablespoons (½ stick) unsalted butter, melted
½ teaspoon freshly grated nutmeg
¼ cup sugar
  3 cups all-purpose flour
  1 tablespoon active dry yeast

Filling

  3 cups fresh cranberries, finely chopped
½ cup dried cranberries, chopped
½ cup chopped pecans or walnuts
¾ cup packed light brown sugar
  2 tablespoons orange marmalade

1. Set your bread machine on the dough cycle or equivalent. Place all the dough ingredients into the bread machine in an order appropriate to your model.
2. Meanwhile, prepare the filling. Place all the filling ingredients in food processor and pulse to combine.
3. Turn the dough out onto a slightly floured surface, divide it into six equal pieces and let it rest for 10 minutes. Roll each piece of the dough into a ¼-inch-thick circle. Place circles on a greased baking sheet and spread a sixth of the filling onto one-half of each circle, leaving a ¼-inch border. Moisten the edges of the circle with water. Fold the unfilled half of the dough over the filling and seal by pressing the edge with the tines of a fork. Cut 2 or 3 vents in the top side of the turnovers. Cover with a kitchen towel and let turnovers rise for about 1 hour, or until puffy.

4. Preheat the oven to 375 degrees F. Bake the turnovers for 15 to 20 minutes, or until golden. Serve hot, warm, or at room temperature.

Serves 6

ORANGE BLOSSOM TEA PUFFS

These diminutive cookielike pastries are crisp on the bottoms and breadlike on top, perfect little bites to nibble with mint tea.

Dough
- ⅓ cup + 2 tablespoons milk
- 1 tablespoon extra virgin olive oil
- 4 tablespoons unsalted butter, melted
- ½ cup sugar
- 1 teaspoon orange blossom water
- 1 teaspoon grated orange zest
- ⅛ teaspoon salt
- 2 cups all-purpose flour
- 1½ teaspoons dry active yeast

Glaze
- ½ cup confectioners' sugar
- 2 tablespoons orange blossom water

1. Set your bread machine on the dough cycle or equivalent. Place all the dough ingredients into the bread machine in an order appropriate to your model.
2. When the cycle is finished, preheat oven to 400 degrees F. Grease a baking sheet. Form dough into flat round mounds, about 2 inches in diameter and ½ inch thick. Place them 1½-inches apart on the prepared baking sheet. Bake for 5 minutes. Immediately lower the heat to 350 degrees F. Bake until the mounds are golden-brown, about 12 to 15 minutes longer. Remove cookies to a wire rack to cool slightly.
3. Meanwhile prepare the glaze. In a small bowl, mix together the confectioners' sugar and orange blossom water until smooth. Spoon some of the glaze over the warm cookies. Let the glaze set for 5 minutes; then spoon another layer on top. Let glaze set for at least 30 minutes before serving.

Makes 1 dozen

NOT TOO SWEET
BREADS

ESPRESSO CHOCOLATE CHIP LOAF

Freezing chocolate chips before adding them to the bread machine keeps them from being pulverized into oblivion by the kneading paddle. It's a tip I picked up from Richard W. Langer's clever book *Bread Machine Sweets and Treats*.

½ cup heavy cream
4 tablespoons (½ stick) unsalted butter, cut into small pieces
1 large egg
2 large egg yolks
1 tablespoon water
1 teaspoon pure vanilla extract
¼ cup sugar
½ teaspoon salt
2½ cups all-purpose flour
2½ active dry yeast
¾ cup chocolate chips, frozen
2 teaspoons ground espresso beans

1. Place all the ingredients, except the chocolate chips and espresso beans, into the bread machine in an order appropriate to your model. If you have the choice, select a raisin or sweet bread with a light crust. Add the chocolate chips and espresso powder when the machine beeps for raisins, or during the last five minutes of the first kneading cycle. When the cycle is finished, immediately turn the bread out of the pan and onto a wire rack to cool completely before serving.

Makes 1 loaf

EASTER KULICH WITH DRIED STRAWBERRIES

Even though the dried strawberries aren't the least bit traditional, they turn this egg-rich loaf pale pink, which makes it all the more fitting for Easter.

Dough
- ½ cup half-and-half or light cream
- 4 tablespoons (½ stick) unsalted butter, cut into small pieces
- 3 large egg yolks
- 1 tablespoon brandy or orange juice
- ½ tablespoon grated lemon zest
- ⅓ cup packed light brown sugar
- ½ teaspoon salt
- 2 cups all-purpose flour
- 2½ teaspoons active dry yeast
- ¼ cup dried strawberries, plumped in boiling water and roughly chopped

Glaze
- 1 cup confectioners' sugar
- 2 tablespoons brandy or orange juice

1. Place all the ingredients, except the strawberries, into the bread machine in an order appropriate to your model. If you have the choice, select a raisin or sweet bread with a light crust. Add the strawberries when the machine beeps for raisins, or during the last five minutes of the first kneading cycle. When the cycle is finished, immediately turn the bread out of the pan and onto a wire rack.

2. Just before the loaf is done baking, prepare the glaze. In a small bowl, mix the confectioners' sugar and brandy together until smooth. Pour the glaze over the top of the loaf, letting it drip down the sides. Let loaf cool completely before serving.

Makes 1 loaf

PAIN D'EPICE WITH LEMON GLAZE

This is a dense, richly flavored gingerbread that can be served with tea, for brunch, or for a sweet lunch when made into cream cheese sandwiches. To serve it for dessert, present a few thin slices of the loaf topped with ripe sugared strawberries, drizzled with Grand Marnier.

Dough
¾ cup milk
6 tablespoons (¾ stick) unsalted butter, softened
1 large egg
¼ cup molasses
¼ cup packed dark brown sugar
1 teaspoon instant espresso powder
1 teaspoon anise seeds
1 teaspoon ground cinnamon
¾ teaspoon ground ginger
¼ teaspoon ground cloves
1 teaspoon salt
2½ cups all-purpose flour
½ cup rye or whole wheat flour
2½ teaspoons active dry yeast
3 tablespoons chopped candied ginger
¾ cup golden raisins
¼ cup chopped prunes

Glaze
1 cup confectioners' sugar
1 tablespoon fresh lemon juice
1 teaspoon grated lemon zest

1. Place all the ingredients, except the candied ginger, raisins, and prunes, into the bread machine in an order appropriate to your model. If you have the choice, select a raisin or sweet bread with a light crust. Add the candied ginger, raisins, and prunes when the machine beeps for raisins, or during the last

five minutes of the first kneading cycle. When the cycle is finished, immediately turn the bread out of the pan and onto a wire rack.

2. Just before the loaf is done baking, prepare the glaze. In a small bowl, mix the confectioners' sugar, lemon juice, and zest together until smooth. Pour the glaze over the top of the loaf, letting it drip down the sides. Let loaf cool completely before serving.

Makes 1 loaf

BANANA MALTED MILK LOAF

Malted milk powder adds a candylike quality to this moist loaf. If you want to use the chocolate-flavored malted milk powder, go ahead, and perhaps add a handful of chocolate chips or malted milk balls after the raisin beep.

1 cup mashed ripe banana (about 2 small)
¼ cup milk
1 tablespoon unsalted butter
1 large egg
1 teaspoon pure vanilla extract
½ cup malted milk powder
⅓ cup packed dark brown sugar
½ teaspoon salt
2¾ cups all-purpose flour
1½ teaspoons active dry yeast

1. Place all the ingredients in the bread machine in an order appropriate to your model. If you have the choice, select a sweet bread with a light crust. When the cycle is finished, immediately turn the bread out of the pan and onto a wire rack to cool completely before slicing.

Makes 1 loaf

BUTTERSCOTCH PEAR BREAD

If you haven't soaked the pears overnight, you can combine them with enough whiskey to cover in a small saucepan, and bring to a boil over low heat. Drain the pears, reserving the whiskey for the dough.

¾ cup (1½ sticks) unsalted butter, softened
2 large eggs
1 large egg yolk
⅓ cup plain yogurt
⅓ cup packed light brown sugar
3 tablespoons whiskey (reserved from the pears)
1 teaspoon salt
3 cups all-purpose flour
1 tablespoon active dry yeast
¾ cup chopped dried pears soaked overnight in whiskey (use the whiskey in the dough)
½ cup butter brickle

1. Place all the ingredients, except the pears and butter brickle, into the bread machine in an order appropriate to your model. If you have the choice, select a raisin or sweet bread with a light crust. Add the pears and butter brickle when the machine beeps for raisins, or during the last five minutes of the first kneading cycle. When the cycle is finished, immediately turn the bread out of the pan and onto a wire rack to cool completely before slicing.

Makes 1 loaf

MRS. ARONSON'S ORANGE JUICE CHALLAH

This recipe comes from Providence, Rhode Island, where my friend Robin Aronson grew up eating her mother's cakey challah during the holidays. Last Rosh Hashanah, Robin made her mother's recipe for my family, and we devoured the loaf, dipped in honey and accompanied by crisp, sliced apples, for one of the sweetest new years we can remember.

½ cup orange juice
¼ cup water
⅓ cup sugar
⅓ cup canola or other flavorless oil
1 teaspoon salt
1 large egg
2 large egg yolks
3 cups all-purpose flour
1 tablespoon active dry yeast
⅓ cup dark raisins, optional

1. Place all the ingredients, except the raisins, in the bread machine in an order appropriate to your model. If you have the choice, select a sweet bread with a light crust. Add the raisins when the machine beeps for them, or during the last five minutes of the first kneading cycle. When the cycle is finished, immediately turn the bread out of the pan and onto a wire rack to cool completely before slicing.

FOR A BRAIDED CHALLAH

To make a traditional braided challah, set the bread machine on the dough cycle, adding the raisins when called for. When the dough is ready, remove it from the pan and divide it in thirds. Form each piece of dough into a rope about 12 inches long, and then braid the ropes together. Place the loaf on a greased cookie sheet, tucking the ends underneath. Make a glaze by beating together an egg with a tablespoon of water. Brush over the top of the loaf. Let the challah rise, uncovered, for 45 minutes. Preheat oven to 375 degrees F. Bake challah until it is a rich golden-brown, about 45 to 50 minutes. Remove to a wire rack to cool completely before serving.

Makes 1 loaf

SWEET CARROT APRICOT BREAD

This is a divine breakfast bread; serve it with cream cheese and apricot jam.

  1 cup grated carrot
½ cup milk
¼ cup canola or other flavorless oil
⅓ cup packed dark brown sugar
  1 teaspoon vanilla extract
  1 teaspoon ground cinnamon
½ teaspoon ground ginger
¼ teaspoon grated nutmeg
½ teaspoon salt
2¼ cups all-purpose flour
1½ teaspoons active dry yeast
½ cup chopped walnuts or pecans
½ cup chopped dried apricots

1. Place all the ingredients, except the nuts and apricots, into the bread machine in an order appropriate to your model. If you have the choice, select a raisin or sweet bread with a light crust. Add the nuts and apricots when the machine beeps for raisins, or during the last five minutes of the first kneading cycle. When the cycle is finished, immediately turn the bread out of the pan and onto a wire rack to cool completely before slicing.

Makes 1 loaf

BLUE BREAD

During the Middle Ages, banquet food was eaten not on individual plates, but piled on large, sturdy slices of bread called *trenchers*. In keeping with the pageantry of a medieval feast, these bread loaves were often brilliantly tinted with saffron, parsley, berries, and flowers. This indigo bread, despite its soft, melting crumb (which is much too delicate to support a morsel of stewed peacock) could have fit right in.

You can buy bilberry or black currant concentrate in large health food stores. If you cannot find it, you may substitute grape concentrate, which is easier to find, and will turn your loaf a lovely burgundy color. You could also substitute dark raisins for the blueberries.

½ cup milk
5 tablespoons unsalted butter, cut into small pieces
3 tablespoons bilberry or black currant concentrate
¼ cup sugar
¼ teaspoon ground allspice
½ teaspoon salt
2 cups all-purpose flour
1½ teaspoons active dry yeast
½ cup dried blueberries, plumped under boiling water, if necessary

1. Place all the ingredients, except the blueberries, into the bread machine in an order appropriate to your model. If you have the choice, select a raisin or sweet bread with a light crust. Add the blueberries when the machine beeps for raisins, or during the last five minutes of the first kneading cycle. When the cycle is finished, immediately turn the bread out of the pan and onto a wire rack to cool completely before slicing.

Makes 1 loaf

ORANGE ALMOND TEA LOAF

This subtle bread has an extremely, soft, moist crumb that comes from the ricotta cheese. It best served the day it is made, and preferably within a few hours of baking. To store any leftovers, wrap well in plastic, refrigerate, and then reheat or toast before serving.

¼ cup milk
¾ cup ricotta cheese
⅓ cup orange marmalade
¼ cup almond paste
1 tablespoon unsalted butter
½ teaspoon almond extract
1 tablespoon orange blossom water
1 tablespoon packed brown sugar
½ teaspoon salt
½ cup ground almonds
2 cups all-purpose flour
1½ teaspoons active dry yeast

1. Place all the ingredients in the bread machine in an order appropriate to your model. If you have the choice, select a sweet bread with a light crust. When the cycle is finished, immediately turn the bread out of the pan and onto a wire rack to cool completely before slicing.

Makes 1 loaf

CHESTNUT HONEY BRIOCHE

Chestnut honey gives this brioche a sweet, musky flavor that is a perfect counterpart to the egg- and butter-rich crumb. However, if you cannot find it, substitute any other type of honey.

The process of adding the butter to the dough after the initial rising is what gives brioche its stupendous texture. The following six brioche recipes are indisputably my favorites in this book and by themselves justify the cost of a bread machine several hundred times over.

    3 large eggs
    2 tablespoons water
    2 tablespoons chestnut honey
  ½ teaspoon salt
    2 cups all-purpose flour
1½ teaspoons active dry yeast
  ¾ cup (1½ sticks) unsalted butter, cut into small pieces

1. Place all the ingredients except the butter in the bread machine in an order appropriate to your model. If you have the choice, select a sweet bread with a light crust. Leave the butter in a warm place to soften while the bread is kneading.
2. When the dough is done with its first rising (this will be at different times in different machines but will generally be about halfway through the cycle), remove the dough from the machine (do not turn it off) and place it with the softened butter in the bowl of a food processor. Pulse the processor on and off until the butter is just incorporated into the dough. This should take about 15 to 30 seconds. Do not overprocess the dough; it doesn't matter if the dough is completely smooth, as long as no large chunks of butter remain visible. If using an electric mixer, mix together the dough and butter at medium speed for about 45 seconds to 1 minute. A food processor is better than a mixer since it works the butter into the dough faster. Return dough to the bread machine (do all this as

quickly as possible) and let the machine finish raising and baking the loaf.

3. When the cycle is finished, immediately turn the bread out of the pan and onto a wire rack to cool completely before slicing.

Makes 1 loaf

CORNMEAL BRIOCHE

For a deliciously juvenile touch, add 1 cup homemade (page 165) or purchased caramel corn to the dough with the butter. Otherwise enjoy this sweet, nutty version of brioche in all of its sophisticated simplicity.

3 large eggs
3 tablespoons water
3 tablespoons sugar
½ teaspoon salt
½ cup yellow cornmeal
1½ cups all-purpose flour
1½ teaspoons active dry yeast
¾ cup (1½ sticks) unsalted butter, cut into small pieces
1 cup caramel corn (page 165), optional

1. Place all the ingredients except the butter (and caramel corn if using) in the bread machine in an order appropriate to your model. If you have the choice, select a sweet bread with a light crust. Leave the butter in a warm place to soften while the bread is kneading.

2. When the dough is done with its first rising (this will be at different times in different machines but will generally be about halfway through the cycle), remove the dough from the machine (do not turn it off) and place it with the softened butter in the bowl of a food processor. Pulse the processor on and off until the butter is just incorporated into the dough. This should take about 15 to 30 seconds. Do not overprocess the dough; it doesn't matter if the dough is completely smooth, as long as no large chunks of butter remain visible. Add the caramel corn if desired and pulse once or twice to distribute it in the dough. If using an electric mixer, mix together the dough and butter at medium speed for about 45 seconds to 1 minute, adding the caramel corn during the last ten seconds. A food processor is better than a mixer since it works the butter into the dough faster. Return dough to the bread ma-

chine (do all this as quickly as possible) and let the machine finish raising and baking the loaf.

3. When the cycle is finished, immediately turn the bread out of the pan and onto a wire rack to cool completely before slicing.

Makes 1 loaf

MAPLE OAT BRIOCHE

Although this brioche does not rise as high as the others, it is no less delicious for its stature. Grade B maple syrup is less delicate than Grade A and therefore has a stronger maple flavor. However, it is harder to find, so you may want to use the maple flavoring to compensate.

  3 **large eggs**
  2 **tablespoons water**
  2 **tablespoons maple syrup, preferably grade B**
  ½ **teaspoon maple flavoring, if desired**
  ½ **teaspoon salt**
  ⅔ **cup rolled oats**
1⅓ **cups all-purpose flour**
1½ **teaspoons active dry yeast**
  ¾ **cup (1½ sticks) unsalted butter, cut into small pieces**

1. Place all the ingredients except the butter in the bread machine in an order appropriate to your model. If you have the choice, select a sweet bread with a light crust. Leave the butter in a warm place to soften while the bread is kneading.
2. When the dough is done with its first rising (this will be at different times in different machines but will generally be about halfway through the cycle), remove the dough from the machine (do not turn it off) and place it with the softened butter in the bowl of a food processor. Pulse the processor on and off until the butter is just incorporated into the dough. This should take about 15 to 30 seconds. Do not overprocess the dough; it doesn't matter if the dough is completely smooth, as long as no large chunks of butter remain visible. If using an electric mixer, mix together the dough and butter at medium speed for about 45 seconds to 1 minute. A food processor is better than a mixer since it works the butter into the dough faster. Return dough to the bread machine (do all this as quickly as possible) and let the machine finish raising and baking the loaf.

3. When the cycle is finished, immediately turn the bread out of the pan and onto a wire rack to cool completely before slicing.

Makes 1 loaf

PRUNE AND ARMAGNAC BRIOCHE

If you neglected to soak your prunes overnight in Armagnac, you can combine them with enough Armagnac to cover in a small saucepan and bring to a boil over low heat. Drain the prunes, reserving the Armagnac for the brioche dough.

3 large eggs
3 tablespoons Armagnac (drained from the prunes)
3 tablespoons sugar
½ teaspoon salt
2 cups all-purpose flour
1½ teaspoons active dry yeast
¾ cup (1½ sticks) unsalted butter, sliced
⅓ cup chopped pitted prunes soaked overnight in
   Armagnac (use the Armagnac for the brioche dough)

1. Place all the ingredients except the butter and prunes in the bread machine in an order appropriate to your model. If you have the choice, select a sweet bread with a light crust. Leave the butter in a warm place to soften while the bread is kneading.

2. When the dough is done with its first rising (this will be at different times in different machines but will generally be about halfway through the cycle), remove the dough from the machine (do not turn it off) and place it with the softened butter in the bowl of a food processor. Pulse the processor on and off until the butter is just incorporated into the dough. This should take about 15 to 30 seconds. Do not overprocess the dough; it doesn't matter if the dough is completely smooth, as long as no large chunks of butter remain visible. Add the prunes and pulse once or twice to distribute them into the dough. If using an electric mixer, mix together the dough and butter at medium speed for about 45 seconds to 1 minute, adding the prunes during the last ten seconds. A food processor is better than a mixer since it works the butter into the dough faster. Return dough to the bread machine (do all this

as quickly as possible) and let the machine finish raising and baking the loaf.

3. When the cycle is finished, immediately turn the bread out of the pan and onto a wire rack to cool completely before slicing.

Makes 1 loaf

PISTACHIO BRIOCHE

Pistachio extract (or essence) is available by mail from La Cuisine and Dean and DeLuca (see the list of sources at the end of this book). If you do not have any, leave it out or substitute almond extract or 1 teaspoon of vanilla. This is a decadent loaf, nubby with the green nuts.

   3 large eggs
   2 tablespoons water
   2 tablespoons honey
   ¼ teaspoon pistachio extract, if desired
   ½ teaspoon salt
   2 cups all-purpose flour
1½ teaspoons active dry yeast
   ¾ cup (1½ sticks) unsalted butter, cut into small pieces
   ½ cup chopped pistachio nuts

1. Place all the ingredients except the butter and pistachio nuts in the bread machine in an order appropriate to your model. If you have the choice, select a sweet bread with a light crust. Leave the butter in a warm place to soften while the bread is kneading.

2. When the dough is done with its first rising (this will be at different times in different machines but will generally be about halfway through the cycle), remove the dough from the machine (do not turn it off) and place it with the softened butter in the bowl of a food processor. Pulse the processor on and off until the butter is just incorporated into the dough. This should take about 15 to 30 seconds. Do not overprocess the dough; it doesn't matter if the dough is completely smooth, as long as no large chunks of butter remain visible. Add the pistachios and pulse once or twice to distribute them into the dough. If using an electric mixer, mix together the dough and butter at medium speed for about 45 seconds to 1 minute, adding the nuts during the last ten seconds. A food processor is better than a mixer since it works the butter into the dough

faster. Return dough to the bread machine (do all this as quickly as possible) and let the machine finish raising and baking the loaf.

3. When the cycle is finished, immediately turn the bread out of the pan and onto a wire rack to cool completely before slicing.

Makes 1 loaf

BROWN SUGAR AND CANDIED GINGER BRIOCHE

If you have candied ginger options, choose the moist kind from Australia, which feels like plump raisins in the mouth but tastes much more electric.

3 large eggs
3 tablespoons water
¼ cup packed dark brown sugar
½ teaspoon salt
2 cups all-purpose flour
1½ teaspoons active dry yeast
¾ cup (1½ sticks) unsalted butter, sliced
⅓ cup chopped candied ginger

1. Place all the ingredients except the butter and ginger in the bread machine in an order appropriate to your model. If you have the choice, select a sweet bread with a light crust. Leave the butter in a warm place to soften while the bread is kneading.

2. When the dough is done with its first rising (this will be at different times in different machines but will generally be about halfway through the cycle), remove the dough from the machine (do not turn it off) and place it with the softened butter in the bowl of a food processor. Pulse the processor on and off until the butter is just incorporated into the dough. This should take about 15 to 30 seconds. Do not overprocess the dough; it doesn't matter if the dough is completely smooth, as long as no large chunks of butter remain visible. Add the ginger and pulse once or twice to distribute it into the dough. If using an electric mixer, mix together the dough and butter at medium speed for about 45 seconds to 1 minute, adding the ginger during the last ten seconds. A food processor is better than a mixer since it works the butter into the dough faster. Return dough to the bread machine (do all this as quickly as possible) and let the machine finish raising and baking the loaf.

3. When the cycle is finished, immediately turn the bread out of the pan and onto a wire rack to cool completely before slicing.

Makes 1 loaf

CHOCOLATE BRIOCHE

This is an extremely rich brioche that is not too sweet. It is a perfect dessert when buttered and spread with raspberry jam, a terrific suggestion given to me by my assistant Malena Watrous.

1 cup semisweet chocolate chips
3 large eggs
5 tablespoons milk
1 teaspoon pure vanilla extract
¼ cup sugar
3 tablespoons unsweetened cocoa powder
½ teaspoon salt
2 cups all-purpose flour
1½ teaspoons active dry yeast
¾ cup (1½ sticks) unsalted butter, cut into small pieces

1. Place all the ingredients except the butter in the bread machine in an order appropriate to your model. If you have the choice, select a sweet bread with a light crust. Leave the butter in a warm place to soften while the bread is kneading.
2. When the dough is done with its first rising (this will be at different times in different machines but will generally be about halfway through the cycle), remove the dough from the machine (do not turn it off) and place it with the softened butter in the bowl of a food processor. Pulse the processor on and off until the butter is just incorporated into the dough. This should take about 15 to 30 seconds. Do not overprocess the dough; it doesn't matter if the dough is completely smooth, as long as no large chunks of butter remain visible. If using an electric mixer, mix together the dough and butter at medium speed for about 45 seconds to 1 minute. A food processor is better than a mixer since it works the butter into the dough faster. Return dough to the bread machine (do all this as quickly as possible) and let the machine finish raising and baking the loaf.

3. When the cycle is finished, immediately turn the bread out of the pan and onto a wire rack to cool completely before slicing.

Makes 1 loaf

BUNS AND SWEET ROLLS

INDIVIDUAL ALMOND KIRSCH CAKES
WITH MARINATED CHERRIES

Although this recipe requires several steps outside the bread machine, including starting with a sponge, the light and tender results are ample compensation for the effort. Serve this dessert at your most important occasion.

If you don't have brandied cherries in your refrigerator, make twice the amount of kirsch syrup and use half for marinating 2 pints of fresh raspberries for several hours. Then serve the raspberries in place of the cherries.

Sponge
- 1 cup milk
- 1 tablespoon sugar
- 1½ cups all-purpose flour
- 1 tablespoon active dry yeast

Dough
- ¾ cup (1½ sticks) unsalted butter, melted
- 2 teaspoons almond extract
- 3 large eggs
- ¾ cup sugar
- 1 teaspoon baking powder
- ½ teaspoon salt
- ¾ cup (3 ounces) ground almonds
- 1¼ cups all-purpose flour

Syrup
- ½ cup sugar
- ⅓ cup kirsch (or substitute brandy or water)
  Grated zest of 1 lemon

For Serving
- 1 recipe brandied cherries (page 181)
  Sweetened whipped cream (use the recipe on page 178, substituting kirsch for the bourbon)

1. To make the sponge, combine in a small saucepan the milk and sugar. Scald the mixture (that is, bring it almost, but not quite, to a boil); then remove pan from the heat. Stir well to cool it down slightly. Add the flour and continue to stir until the flour is incorporated. When the mixture feels warm, but not hot, stir in the yeast. Let the sponge develop in a warm spot for 1 hour.

2. Set your bread machine on the dough cycle or equivalent. Add the sponge and then the remaining dough ingredients, placing them in an order that is appropriate to your model. The sponge counts as a liquid.

3. When the cycle is complete, remove dough from the machine and divide it into 18 balls. Place the balls in greased muffin tins, cover with plastic wrap, and let rise for 25 minutes.

4. Meanwhile, prepare the syrup. In a small saucepan over medium-high heat, combine the sugar, kirsch, and lemon zest. Cook the mixture, stirring, until the sugar dissolves, about 3 minutes. Remove pan from the heat.

5. Preheat oven to 350 degrees F. Bake the cakes until they are golden-brown on top, about 20 to 25 minutes. Remove tins from the oven and place on a wire rack. Using a fork, poke each cake several times to create hollows for the syrup to seep into. While the cakes are still warm, brush generously with the syrup. Let cool completely before slicing the cakes in half horizontally and serving with the brandied cherries and whipped cream on top, like a grown-up shortcake.

Serves 12

VALENCIA SWEET BUNS

These spongy buns are typically served for breakfast, with good, strong coffee, in many parts of Spain. The combination of olive oil, sherry, and cinnamon are typically and deliciously Spanish.

Dough
½ cup milk
1 large egg
1 large egg yolk
⅓ cup sugar
3 tablespoons unsalted butter, cut into bits
2 tablespoons extra virgin olive oil
1 tablespoon cream sherry
¼ teaspoon ground cinnamon
¼ teaspoon salt
2 cups all-purpose flour
2 teaspoons active dry yeast
3 tablespoons golden raisins

Topping
1 large egg white, beaten stiff
2 teaspoons sugar

1. Set your bread machine on the dough cycle or equivalent. Add all the dough ingredients (except the raisins) placing them in an order that is appropriate to your model. Add the raisins when the machine beeps or during the last 5 minutes of the first kneading cycle.
2. When the cycle is complete, remove dough from the machine and divide it into 14 balls. Place the balls two inches apart on greased baking trays, cover with plastic wrap, and let rise for 1½ hours at room temperature, or overnight in the refrigerator.
3. Preheat oven to 325 degrees F. Using a small spatula or

knife, spread the egg white in a thin layer over the buns. Sprinkle with the sugar. Bake the buns until they are golden-brown around the edges, about 25 minutes.

Makes 14

MEDIEVAL SPICED CREAM BUNS

These buns are flavored with rose water, orange blossom water, and ground spices, which echo the taste combinations favored during the Middle Ages.

Dough

- ½ cup milk
- 5 tablespoons unsalted butter, cut into small pieces
- 1 tablespoon rose water
- 1 tablespoon orange blossom water
- 1 tablespoon fresh lemon juice
- ¼ cup sugar
- ½ teaspoon salt
- 2 cups all-purpose flour
- 1½ teaspoons active dry yeast

Filling

- 7 ounces (half 14-ounce can) sweetened condensed milk
- ½ teaspoon ground cinnamon
- ½ teaspoon ground ginger
  Pinch of ground cloves
- 1 large egg yolk

1. Set your bread machine on the dough cycle or equivalent. Add all the dough ingredients, placing them in an order that is appropriate to your model.
2. While the dough is still in the machine, prepare the filling. In a small bowl, combine all the filling ingredients, mixing very well. Reserve.
3. When the cycle is complete, remove dough from the machine and roll it on a floured surface into a 12 × 15–inch rectangle. Spread with ¾ of the filling, reserving the rest. Starting with a short side, roll the dough up, jelly-roll style. Cut dough into 8 buns. Place the buns, seam side down, two inches apart on greased baking trays, cover with plastic wrap, and let rise for 1 hour at room temperature.

4. Preheat oven to 350 degrees F. Brush the buns with the remaining filling mixture. Bake until the buns are golden-brown, about 18 minutes.

Makes 8

CARDAMOM-SAFFRON BUNS

The large beads of pearl sugar topping these fragrant buns are available in speciality stores like Williams-Sonoma. If you can't find them, substitute demarara (raw, unrefined) sugar, which will supply the needed crunch.

When using cardamom, picking the little black seeds from the pods and grinding them by hand (a mortar and pestle are good if you don't have a spice grinder) may be time-consuming, but the flavor is so much better than using the preground stuff, which gets bitter over time. If you must use the powder, make sure it is fresh.

Dough
- ¼ teaspoon saffron strands, crumbled
- ½ cup milk
- ¼ cup water
- 4 tablespoons (½ stick) unsalted butter, melted
- 2 large eggs
- ⅓ cup sugar
- 1 teaspoon cardamom seeds, ground
- 1 teaspoon salt
- 3 cups all-purpose flour
- 2 tablespoons active dry yeast
- 1½ cups golden raisins

Topping
- 1 large egg, beaten well
- Pearl sugar

1. In a small saucepan, combine the saffron and milk over medium heat. Bring the mixture to a boil, then remove pan from the heat.
2. Set your bread machine on the dough cycle or equivalent. Add all the dough ingredients including the saffron-milk, placing them in an order that is appropriate to your model.
3. When the cycle is complete, remove dough and divide into

18 pieces. Flour the palms of your hands and roll each piece lightly into a rough bun shape. Place the buns two inches apart on greased baking sheets. Cover with plastic wrap and let rise for 30 minutes, or until doubled in volume.

4. Preheat oven to 375 degrees F. Brush the buns with the beaten egg and sprinkle well with the pearl sugar. Bake for 15 to 20 minutes, or until golden-brown.

Makes 18

GLAZED CHELSEA BUNS

This is based on an eighteenth-century British recipe that much resembles a simplified version of honey buns.

Dough
½ cup milk
1 tablespoon unsalted butter
1 large egg
1 tablespoon sugar
½ teaspoon salt
1½ cups all-purpose flour
2 teaspoons active dry yeast

Filling and Glaze
2 tablespoons unsalted butter, melted
1 cup chopped mixed dried fruit (such as raisins, currants, prunes, apricots, pears, dates, figs, cranberries, etc., soaked in hot tea if the fruit is leathery)
¼ cup finely chopped mixed candied citrus rind
⅓ cup packed light brown sugar
Honey, to glaze

1. Set your bread machine on the dough cycle or equivalent. Add all the dough ingredients, placing them in an order that is appropriate to your model.
2. Grease a 9-inch square cake pan. When the cycle is complete, remove the dough from the machine and roll it out to a 10 × 14–inch rectangle. Brush with the melted butter and sprinkle with the dried fruit, citrus rind, and brown sugar, but only to within ½ inch of the edges.
3. Starting from a long side, roll up the dough like a jelly roll and pinch the edges together. Cut the roll into 9 equal slices and place, cut side down, in the greased pan, three in a row. Cover the pan with plastic wrap and let buns rise for about 30 minutes, or until doubles in size.

4. Preheat the oven to 375 degrees. Bake buns for about 25 to 30 minutes, or until the top is golden-brown. Turn out onto a wire rack and, while still warm, brush with honey for a shiny, sticky glaze.

Makes 9

RED BEAN PASTE BUNS

Sweetened red bean paste adds a smoky, rich flavor to these delicious breakfast buns, which are best served with Lapsang Souchong tea. It is available in Asian markets and some very large supermarkets.

Dough
- ¾ cup milk
- 4 tablespoons (½ stick) unsalted butter, cut into small pieces
- ½ teaspoon almond extract
- ⅓ cup sweetened red bean paste
- 2 tablespoons packed dark brown sugar
- ½ teaspoon salt
- 2⅓ cups all-purpose flour
- 1½ teaspoons active dry yeast

Filling
- 2 tablespoons unsalted butter, melted
- ¼ cup packed dark brown sugar
- 2 tablespoons ground almonds

1. Set your bread machine on the dough cycle or equivalent. Add all the dough ingredients, placing them in an order that is appropriate to your model.

2. When the cycle is complete, remove the dough from the machine and roll it out to a 10 × 14–inch rectangle. Brush with the melted butter and sprinkle with the brown sugar and almonds but only to within ½ inch of the edges.

3. Starting with a long side, roll up the dough like a jelly roll and pinch the edges together. Cut the roll into 9 equal slices and place, seam side down, two inches apart on a greased baking tray. Cover the buns with plastic wrap and let rise for about 45 minutes.

4. Preheat the oven to 375 degrees. Bake buns for about 20 minutes, or until their tops are golden-brown. Remove tray to a wire rack to cool.

Makes 9

LITCHI BUNS

For this recipe, if you have a choice, pick the soft type of almond paste sold either in bulk or in cans. Litchis are available in large supermarkets, and of course, Asian markets.

Dough
   1 cup canned litchis with liquid
   3 tablespoons unsalted butter
   1 egg
   ½ teaspoon pure vanilla extract
   ¼ teaspoon almond extract
   ¼ cup sugar
   ½ teaspoon salt
   2½ cups all-purpose flour
   1½ teaspoons active dry yeast

Filling
   ⅓ cup almond paste

1. Set your bread machine on the dough cycle or equivalent. Add all the dough ingredients, placing them in an order that is appropriate to your model.
2. When the cycle is over, remove dough from the machine and divide it into 12 portions and fit them into greased muffin tins. Cover with plastic and let rise for 30 minutes.
3. Preheat oven to 350 degrees F. Divide the almond paste into 12 equal pieces and form into balls. Using a finger, make an indentation in the center of each bun (remove the plastic first) and sink an almond paste ball into the hole. Bake buns until they are golden, about 15 minutes. Remove pan from the oven and let buns cool on a wire rack before serving.

Makes 12

COCONUT-PEANUT BUNS

One critic of my first bread machine cookbook wrote that some of the ingredients I use are hard to find. This is true, but for me, shopping in exotic markets is part of the fun. Peanut powder is sold in Asian markets in small packets or tins to be mixed up with water and served as a hot beverage. Instead, I use it as the base for a filling for these rich buns, which are reminiscent of treats from the dim sum cart.

Dough
- ¾ cup milk
- 1 large egg
- 2 tablespoons molasses
- 4 tablespoons (½ stick) unsalted butter
- 2 tablespoons sugar
- ¾ teaspoon salt
- 2½ cups all-purpose flour
- 2½ teaspoons active dry yeast

Filling
- ¼ cup unsweetened coconut milk
- ⅔ cup peanut powder
- ½ cup shredded unsweetened coconut
- 2 tablespoons all-purpose flour

Topping
- 1 large egg yolk
- 1 tablespoon water

1. Set your bread machine on the dough cycle or equivalent. Add all the dough ingredients, placing them in an order that is appropriate to your model.
2. Meanwhile, prepare the filling. In a small bowl, combine the filling ingredients and mix well. Place filling in the refrigerator until the dough is ready.

3. When the cycle is complete, remove the dough from the machine and roll it out to a 14-inch square. Cut the dough into 8 equal smaller squares. Place a tablespoon of filling in the center of each square and bring the edges up to enclose the filling, twisting them to seal. Place the buns, twisted side down, two inches apart on a greased baking tray. Cover the buns with plastic wrap and let rise for about 45 minutes.

4. Preheat the oven to 375 degrees. In a small bowl, combine the egg yolk and water, mixing well. Uncover the buns and brush them with the egg mixture. Bake buns for about 18 minutes, or until the tops are golden-brown. Remove tray to a wire rack to cool.

Makes 8

BITE-SIZE DATE AND COCONUT TAMARIND BUNS

The key ingredient for these buns, the date-coconut balls, are available in most health food stores or large candy and nut shops. I've also found them in large supermarkets. They are made of date paste rolled in coconut and topped with a blanched almond. If you can't find them, simply substitute a mixture of 1½ cups dates and ½ cup unsweetened shredded coconut mashed in a food processor.

The tamarind concentrate is a thick, inky liquid sold in Middle Eastern and Latin-American shops, or by mail from Kalustyan. You can, however, leave it out, or substitute ½ teaspoon ground cinnamon for a different flavor.

Dough
   ½ cup milk
   2 large eggs
   4 tablespoons (½ stick) unsalted butter
   ⅓ cup brown sugar
   ¼ teaspoon tamarind concentrate
   1 teaspoon salt
2⅓ cups all-purpose flour
   2 teaspoons active dry yeast

Filling
   2 cups date coconut balls

1. Set your bread machine on the dough cycle or equivalent. Add all the dough ingredients, placing them in an order that is appropriate to your model.
2. Meanwhile, prepare the filling. In a small bowl, mash the date coconut balls with a fork, or place in a food processor and process until mushy.
3. When the cycle is complete, remove the dough from the machine and roll it out to a 20-inch square. Cut the dough into 16 equal smaller squares. Place a teaspoon of filling in

the center of each square and bring the edges up to enclose the filling, twisting them to seal. Place the buns, twisted side down, two inches apart on a greased baking tray. Cover the buns with plastic wrap and let rise for about 45 minutes.

4. Preheat the oven to 375 degrees. Bake buns for about 18 minutes, or until the tops are golden-brown. Remove tray to a wire rack to cool.

Makes 16

NUTELLA CREAM BUNS

Nutella is a thick, sticky hazelnut-chocolate spread that I used to eat spread on bread as a child. Now I eat it straight from the jar. It is available in gourmet shops.

Dough

½ cup heavy cream
3 tablespoons unsalted butter
¼ cup sugar
3 tablespoons orange juice
Grated zest of one small orange
½ teaspoon salt
½ cup finely chopped, toasted hazelnuts
2 cups all-purpose flour
2 teaspoons active dry yeast

Filling

¾ cup nutella
1 large egg
1 teaspoon pure vanilla extract

1. Set your bread machine on the dough cycle or equivalent. Add all the dough ingredients, placing them in an order that is appropriate to your model. Add the hazelnuts with all the other ingredients, not during the raisin cycle if your machine has one.

2. Meanwhile, prepare the filling. In a small bowl, mix together the Nutella, egg, and vanilla, stirring until smooth.

3. When the cycle is complete, remove the dough from the machine and roll it out to a 14-inch square. Cut the dough into 12 equal smaller squares. Place a heaping teaspoon of filling in the center of each square and bring the edges up to enclose the filling, twisting them to seal. Place the buns, twisted side down, into buttered muffin tins. Cover the buns with plastic wrap and let rise for about 45 minutes.

4. Preheat the oven to 350 degrees. Bake buns for about 15 to 18 minutes, or until the tops are golden-brown. Remove muffin tray to a wire rack to cool.

Makes 12

RASPBERRY ALMOND HONEY BUNS

Flavored honeys, including those mixed with raspberries, orange, cranberries, and blueberries, are a delicious innovation. They are easily found in large supermarkets.

Dough
- ¼ cup plus 2 tablespoons water
- ¼ cup milk
- 4 tablespoons (½ stick) unsalted butter
- 2 large eggs
- 1 teaspoon pure vanilla extract
- 3 tablespoons sugar
- ½ teaspoon salt
- 2½ cups all-purpose flour
- 1½ teaspoons active dry yeast

Topping
- ⅓ cup packed light brown sugar
- 1 tablespoon unsalted butter, melted
- ¼ cup ground almonds
- ¼ cup currants, plumped in boiling water if necessary
- 1 teaspoon ground cinnamon
- ⅛ teaspoon grated nutmeg
- ⅛ teaspoon ground cloves

Syrup
- ½ cup raspberry honey
- 6 tablespoons unsalted butter
- 2 tablespoons packed brown sugar

1. Set your bread machine on the dough cycle or equivalent. Add all the dough ingredients, placing them in an order that is appropriate to your model.
2. Meanwhile prepare the filling. Combine all the topping ingredients in the bowl of a food processor and process until a paste forms. Reserve. To prepare the syrup, butter a 9 × 13–

inch baking pan generously. In a small saucepan, combine the syrup ingredients over low heat and cook them, stirring, until they are melted and smooth. Pour the syrup into the buttered pan.

3. When the cycle is complete, remove the dough from the machine and roll it out to a 12 × 16–inch rectangle. Carefully spread dough with the filling to within ½ an inch of the edges.

4. Roll up the dough from the longest side and pinch the edges together. Cut the roll into 12 equal slices and place, cut side down, in the syruped pan. Cover the pan with plastic wrap and let buns rise for about 45 minutes, or until doubled in size.

5. Preheat the oven to 350 degrees. Bake buns for about 25 to 30 minutes, or until the top has turned a rich golden-brown. Invert the pan onto a platter; carefully lift off the pan. Cool buns to lukewarm. Pull apart and serve.

Makes 12 buns

CORNMEAL CAJETA PIÑON BUNS

Cajeta is essentially a caramel sauce made either from goat's or cow's milk. I always prefer the one made from goat's milk, which has a slightly pungent quality. It is available in Latin-American and some Philippine markets, or, you can make your own (page 177). If you don't have piñon (pine nuts, pignoli) substitute slivered almonds.

Dough
⅓ **cup buttermilk**
¾ **cups (1½ sticks) unsalted butter, softened**
3 **eggs**
⅓ **cup sugar**
1 **teaspoon salt**
1 **cup yellow cornmeal**
1 **cup all-purpose flour**
1 **tablespoon active dry yeast**

Filling
¾ **cup cajeta (see page 177)**
1 **large egg**
½ **cup piñon nuts, chopped**

Topping
2 **tablespoons unsalted butter, melted**
2 **tablespoons piñon nuts**

1. Set your bread machine on the dough cycle or equivalent. Add all the dough ingredients, placing them in an order that is appropriate to your model.
2. Meanwhile, in a small bowl, mix together the cajeta and the egg.
3. When the cycle is complete, remove the dough from the machine and roll it out to a 10 × 14–inch rectangle. Spread with the cajeta mixture to within ½ inch of the edges, and then sprinkle cajeta with the chopped pinons.

4. Roll up the dough from the longest side and pinch the edges together. Cut the roll into 9 equal slices and place, seam side down, two inches apart on a greased baking tray. Cover the buns with plastic wrap and let rise for about 45 minutes.

5. Preheat the oven to 375 degrees. Brush buns with the butter; then sprinkle on the remaining 2 tablespoons piñon nuts. Bake buns for about 18 minutes, or until the tops are golden-brown. Remove tray to a wire rack to cool.

Makes 9

CAKES AND COFFEE
CAKES

MORAVIAN SWEET POTATO
SUGAR CAKE

This is my twist on a classic Moravian sugar cake, which consists of an enriched dough made from potatoes, then slathered with an extravagant butter and brown sugar topping. I use sweet potatoes, which have the dual advantage of being easily prepared (canned yams, even canned candied yams, work perfectly) and adding a rich butterscotch flavor to the dough (not to mention a pretty pumpkin color).

This cake is good picnic fare. Or serve it warm for dessert, à la mode with a drizzle of caramel sauce (page 176).

Dough

- ½ cup milk
- 6 tablespoons (¾ stick) unsalted butter, melted and cooled slightly
- ⅔ cup mashed sweet potato (canned or candied yams, are fine)
- 2 large eggs
- ¼ cup sugar
- ½ teaspoon salt
- 3 cups all-purpose flour
- 1 tablespoon active dry yeast

Topping

- ½ cup packed light brown sugar
- 1½ teaspoons ground cinnamon
- 4 tablespoons (½ stick) unsalted butter, melted and cooled slightly
- ½ cup heavy cream

1. Place all the dough ingredients, in an order that is appropriate to your model, in your bread machine set for the dough cycle. At the end of the cycle, transfer the dough to to a lightly greased 12 × 17–inch baking pan. Let it rest for 10 minutes.

2. Using a rolling pin and/or your hands, press the dough into the pan. Cover it with a damp dish towel (plastic wrap tends to stick to the dough) and set it aside to rise until doubled in bulk, about 1 hour.

3. Preheat oven to 400 degrees F. To make the topping, mix the sugar and cinnamon together in a small bowl. Using your fingertips, the end of a thin wooden spoon, or the larger end of a chopstick, gently create dimples in the dough. Drizzle the dough with the melted butter, sprinkle with the cinnamon sugar, then drizzle heavy cream over all. Bake the cake until it is golden-brown and bubbling, about 15 to 20 minutes. Remove it from the oven and cool it completely on a wire rack.

Serves 8–10

PUMPKIN PECAN COFFEE RING WITH MAPLE GLAZE

This moist, sugary-glazed cake is a brunch favorite. While it is best served freshly made and still a bit warm, it can also be frozen and reheated with great results.

Dough
- ¾ cup milk
- 4 tablespoons (½ stick) unsalted butter, cut into small pieces
- ⅓ cup mashed pumpkin (canned is fine)
- 1 teaspoon pure vanilla extract
- ¼ cup packed dark brown sugar
- ½ teaspoon salt
- ¼ cup ground pecans
- 2½ cups all-purpose flour
- 1½ teaspoons active dry yeast

Filling
- 2 tablespoons unsalted butter, melted
- ¼ cup packed dark brown sugar
- 2 tablespoons ground pecans

Glaze
- ½ cup confectioners' sugar
- 1½ tablespoons pure maple syrup

1. Set your bread machine on the dough cycle or equivalent. Add all the dough ingredients, placing them in an order that is appropriate to your model.
2. When the cycle is complete, remove the dough from the machine and roll it out to a 12 × 26–inch rectangle. Brush with the melted butter and sprinkle with the brown sugar and pecans to within ½ inch of the edges.
3. Starting with a long side, roll up the dough tightly, jelly-roll style. Shape dough into a ring, pinching the ends together

to seal; place it seam side down on a greased baking sheet. Using scissors, make crosswise cuts into the top of the dough at ½-inch intervals, cutting about halfway through the cake. Pull cut sections a little bit out to opposite sides, away from each other; they should be overlapping. Cover the ring with plastic wrap and let rise until almost doubled, about 45 minutes.

4. Preheat the oven to 375 degrees F. Bake ring for about 25 minutes, or until the top is golden-brown. Remove tray to a wire rack to cool slightly.

5. Meanwhile, prepare the glaze by mixing the confectioners' sugar and maple syrup together until smooth. Drizzle glaze over the top of the cake. Let glaze set for at least 20 minutes before serving.

Serves 8

COCONUT LIME CAKE WITH BANANAS

This cake is the one I think of when layered, birthday-style cakes are required. It is composed of two moist layers sandwiching sliced bananas nestled in curd or whipped cream and then glazed with lime marmalade. What could be better?

¾ cup milk or unsweetened coconut milk
3 large eggs
3 tablespoons unsalted butter, cut into bits
2 tablespoons fresh lime juice
Grated zest of 2 limes
½ teaspoon baking powder
½ teaspoon salt
3 cups all-purpose flour
1½ teaspoons active dry yeast
½ cup shredded unsweetened coconut

Filling
1 recipe lime curd (page 167) or 1 cup heavy cream, whipped
2 large ripe bananas, sliced

Glaze
½ cup lime marmalade (or substitute orange, lemon, or ginger), stirred well

1. Set your bread machine on the dough cycle or equivalent. Add all the dough ingredients, except for the coconut, placing them in an order that is appropriate to your model. Add the coconut when the machine beeps for raisins or during the last 5 minutes of the first kneading. Grease and flour a 9-inch cake pan.
2. When the cycle is finished, transfer the dough to the pan. Cover pan with plastic wrap and let rise until doubled in size, about 1 hour.

3. Preheat oven to 350 degrees F. Bake cake until a metal skewer inserted in the center comes out dry (a few crumbs are okay), about 35 to 40 minutes. If it begins to brown too rapidly, cover the top with foil. Remove pan from the oven and turn the cake onto a wire rack to cool. While the cake is still warm, brush the top with the glaze.

4. To serve, split the cake into two layers, then fill with the whipped cream and bananas.

Serves 8–10

CHOCOLATE CHIP BUTTERSCOTCH PUDDING CAKE

This cake is another one of those layer-style birthday beauties, this time created for the chocolate lover. For a double chocolate treat, substitute mocha custard filling (page 172) or chocolate pudding for the butterscotch pudding.

Dough
- ⅔ cup milk
- 2 large eggs
- 3 tablespoons unsalted butter, cut into small pieces
- 2 teaspoons pure vanilla extract
- ⅓ cup sugar
- ⅓ cup unsweetened cocoa powder
- ½ teaspoon salt
- 2½ cups all-purpose flour
- 2 teaspoons active dry yeast
- ⅔ cup chocolate chips

Filling and Topping
- 1 recipe butterscotch pudding (page 171)
  Confectioners' sugar, for sprinkling

1. Set your bread machine on the dough cycle or equivalent. Add all the dough ingredients, placing them in an order that is appropriate to your model. Grease and flour a 9-inch cake pan.
2. When the cycle is finished, transfer the dough into the pan. Cover pan with plastic wrap and let rise until doubled in size, about 1 hour.
3. Preheat oven to 350 degrees F. Bake cake until a metal skewer inserted in the center comes out dry (a few crumbs are okay), about 35 to 40 minutes. If it begins to brown too rapidly, cover the top with foil. Remove pan from the oven and turn the cake onto a wire rack to cool.

4. To serve, split the cake into two layers, fill with the butterscotch pudding, and sprinkle the top with confectioners' sugar.

Serves 8

MAPLE WALNUT COFFEE RING

An extremely sticky, syrup-oozing cake. While this is not a dessert for the ultra-refined, kids and sweet-toothed adults will love it. Being of the latter, I like it a lot.

Dough
- ½ cup milk
- ¼ cup pure maple syrup
- 2 tablespoons unsalted butter, cut into small pieces
- 2 large eggs
- 1 teaspoon salt
- 2½ cups all-purpose flour
- 2 teaspoons active dry yeast

Topping and Glaze
- 1 cup toasted walnuts, chopped
- ¾ cup pure maple syrup
- 6 tablespoons (½ stick) unsalted butter, melted and cooled

1. Set your bread machine on the dough cycle or equivalent. Add all the dough ingredients, placing them in an order that is appropriate to your model.

2. Make the topping by mixing together the walnuts and ½ of the maple syrup in a small saucepan and simmering for 10 minutes.

3. Lightly grease a 13 × 9–inch pan. Divide the dough into 24 small pieces and roll each piece into a ball. Dip the balls in the melted butter; then place them in the prepared pan and flatten slightly. Reserve the remaining butter. Spoon the topping over and around the dough. Cover the pan with a damp dish towel and let rise until doubled in bulk, about 1 hour.

4. Preheat oven to 350 degrees F. Bake the cake for 30 minutes, or until golden-brown and bubbling. If the top gets too brown before the cake is done, cover it with a piece of foil.

5. While the cake is baking, prepare the glaze. In a small saucepan, combine the remaining butter and maple syrup. Bring to a boil, stirring, then remove pan from the heat and set aside. Remove the cake from the oven and turn it out onto a wire rack; scrape any remaining topping out of the pan and spread it over the cake. Pull the cake apart slightly into buns and drizzle them with the glaze. Let glaze set for at least 15 minutes before serving.

Serves 8–10

WHITE CHOCOLATE POPPY SEED
COFFEE SPIRAL

The muskiness of poppy seeds tempers the generally cloying sweetness of white chocolate in this strudel-like loaf.

Dough
 ⅔ cup milk
 ¼ cup sour cream
 1 large egg
 2 tablespoons unsalted butter, cut into small pieces
 ¼ cup sugar
 ½ teaspoon salt
2½ cups all-purpose flour
 2 teaspoons active dry yeast

Filling
 ¼ cup poppy seeds
 3 tablespoons cream cheese
 2 ounces white chocolate, melted
1½ tablespoon heavy cream
 1 large egg

Glaze
 1 large egg, well beaten

1. Set your bread machine on the dough cycle or equivalent. Add all the dough ingredients, placing them in an order that is appropriate to your model.
2. Meanwhile prepare the filling by combining the poppy seeds, cream cheese, white chocolate, heavy cream, and egg in the bowl of a food processor fitted with a steel blade. Process the mixture until it is smooth, about 30 seconds.
3. When the cycle is complete, remove the dough from the machine and roll it out to a 12 × 16–inch rectangle. Spread with the filling to within ½ inch of the edges. Starting with a short side, roll up the dough tightly, jelly-roll style. Place it,

seam side down, onto a greased baking sheet. Cover the loaf with plastic wrap and let rise until almost doubled, about 45 minutes.

4. Preheat the oven to 375 degrees F. Brush top of the loaf with the glaze. Bake loaf for about 20 to 25 minutes, or until the top is golden brown. Remove tray to a wire rack to cool slightly.

Serves 6

KUGELHOPF

Sometimes spelled Gugelhopf, this buttery cake finds its origins in Alsace, a region in France abutting the border of Germany. It is a lovely, feathery-textured cake that is just right with tea or coffee, although it is perhaps too airy to dunk without falling to crumbs in your cup.

If you haven't soaked your raisins in rum overnight, bring them to a simmer in a small saucepan; then remove the pan from the heat. Let raisins steep for 15 minutes before proceeding with the recipe.

Dough
- ¾ cup whole milk
- 2 large eggs
- 4 tablespoons (½ stick) unsalted butter, cut into small pieces
- ½ cup sugar
- 1½ teaspoons grated lemon zest
- ¼ teaspoon salt
- 2½ cups all-purpose flour
- 1 tablespoon active dry yeast
- ½ cup golden raisins soaked overnight in ¼ cup dark rum

Topping
- 1 tablespoon unsalted butter, melted
- ¼ cup ground almonds
- 1 tablespoon turbinado (demerara or raw) sugar
- 18 to 20 whole blanched almonds
  Confectioners' sugar, to dust

1. Set your bread machine on the dough cycle or equivalent. Add all the dough ingredients except the raisins, placing them in an order that is appropriate to your model. Add the raisins and their liquid when the machine beeps for them, or during the last five minutes of the first kneading cycle.

2. Meanwhile, thoroughly coat a 1½-quart tube mold or a 10-inch angel food cake pan with the melted butter. Shake the pan or mold to coat the lower two-thirds of the sides with the finely ground almonds and the turbinado sugar. Arrange the whole almonds in an attractive pattern on the bottom of the pan.

3. Transfer the dough (it will be soft and batterlike) into the mold or pan—without disturbing the almonds. Spoons are good for this, or use your hands. Cover pan with plastic wrap and let rise until doubled in size, about 1 to 1½ hours.

4. Preheat oven to 350 degrees F. Bake kugelhopf until a metal skewer inserted in the center comes out dry (a few crumbs are okay), about 45 minutes. If it begins to brown too rapidly, cover the top with foil; the top should only bake to a light golden-brown. Remove pan from the oven and turn the cake onto a wire rack to cool. Just before serving, dust lightly with confectioners' sugar.

Serves 6–8

GOLDEN DUMPLING RING WITH PEARS

This Eastern European dumpling cake is typically served with midafternoon coffee, indulgently capped with whipped cream. After a snack like that, who needs dinner?

Dough
- ¼ cup milk
- ¼ cup heavy cream
- 4 tablespoons (½ stick) unsalted butter, cut into small pieces
- 2 large eggs
- ⅓ cup packed light brown sugar
- 1 teaspoon salt
- 2⅓ cups all-purpose flour
- 2 teaspoons active dry yeast

Filling
- ¾ cup toasted hazelnuts, skins rubbed off with a dish towel (see note)
- ½ stick unsalted butter, softened
- ½ cup confectioners' sugar
- 1 teaspoon ground ginger
- ½ cup chopped dried pears (plumped in boiling water if necessary)

Glaze
- 1 cup confectioners' sugar
- 2 tablespoons brewed tea, coffee, or water

1. Set your bread machine on the dough cycle or equivalent. Add all the dough ingredients, placing them in an order that is appropriate to your model.

2. Make the filling. Place the hazelnuts, butter, confectioners' sugar, and ginger in the bowl of a food processor fitted with a steel blade. Process until a paste is formed, about 60 seconds. Pulse in the chopped dried pears.

3. When the cycle is complete, remove the dough from the machine and let it rest in a bowl for 10 minutes. Grease and flour a 10-inch tube or Bundt pan. On a lightly floured surface, roll dough into a 12 × 12–inch square, then cut it into 16 equal pieces. Place 1 tablespoon of the filling in the center of each square of dough. Lift the corners of each square, pinching them together to enclose the filling.

4. Place half the dumplings, seam side up, in the bottom of the pan, spacing them evenly. Place the remaining dumplings, seam side down, between the dumplings on the bottom. Cover pan with plastic and let rise until almost doubled, about 1 hour.

5. Preheat the oven to 375 degrees F. Bake the cake until it is golden brown, about 40 minutes. Remove it from the oven and let cool on a wire rack.

6. Meanwhile prepare the glaze. In a small bowl, mix together the confectioners' sugar and liquid of choice until smooth. Spoon it onto the coffee ring, letting any excess drip down the sides.

Serves 6–8

Note: To toast hazelnuts, spread them out on a baking sheet and bake at 350 degrees F for about 15 minutes or until the skins parch and begin to flake off. Then, working with a few at a time, rub them together in a dish towel so that most of the skin flakes off. Pick out the nuts and discard the skins. Don't worry about the few little pieces of skin tenaciously stuck to the nut.

HONEY LOAF WITH PIGNOLIA AND PRUNES

This is a traditional Italian holiday loaf that finds its origins in the cooking of ancient Rome, where honey was the only sweetener. It is a satisfyingly sticky, dense loaf loaded with honey, dried fruit, and nuts, then baked and glazed with even more honey. Keep napkins within reach.

Dough
- ½ **cup milk**
- ¼ **cup water**
- 2 **tablespoons honey**
- 2 **tablespoons unsalted butter, melted and cooled**
- 1 **tablespoon extra virgin olive oil**
- 1 **large egg yolk, at room temperature**
- 1 **teaspoon anise seeds**
- 2 **teaspoons grated lemon zest**
- ½ **teaspoon salt**
- 2½ **cups all-purpose flour**
- 1½ **teaspoons active dry yeast**

Filling and Glaze
- ⅓ **cup sliced blanched almonds**
- ⅓ **cup finely chopped and pitted prunes**
- ¼ **cup golden raisins**
- 2 **tablespoons pignolia (pine nuts)**
- 5 **tablespoons honey**

1. Set your bread machine on the dough cycle or equivalent. Add all the dough ingredients, placing them in an order that is appropriate to your model. When the cycle is complete, turn the machine off and let dough rise for 45 minutes in the bread machine pan.
2. Meanwhile prepare the filling. In a small bowl, mix the almonds, prunes, raisins, and pignolia. Set aside.

3. Punch the dough down (it will be sticky) and turn it out onto a well-floured surface. Knead for 2 minutes, then pinch off an egg-sized piece of dough and set aside. With a rolling pin, roll the remaining dough out into a 10 × 14–inch rectangle. With a brush, spread 4 tablespoons of the honey over the dough. Reserve 3 tablespoons of the filling and sprinkle the remainder evenly over the dough. Starting with a long side, roll the dough up as for a jelly roll. Place the roll on a lightly greased large baking sheet and set aside.

4. Roll the remaining piece of dough into a 6-inch square and cut out ten ½-inch strips with a decorative pastry wheel or sharp knife. Make 5 crisscross designs on top of the bread using 2 strips each. Tuck the ends underneath the loaf. Cover with plastic and let loaf rise until doubled in size, about 30 minutes.

5. Preheat the oven to 350 degrees F. Bake loaf for 30 to 35 minutes, or until the bread is golden-brown. Remove immediately to a cooling rack. With a brush, spread the remaining tablespoon of honey over the top of the loaf and sprinkle on the remaining filling. Let the bread cool before serving.

Serves 6–8

PISTACHIO ROSE BRAID

This is a marvelous bread, with its green-flecked pistachio dough enriched with sour cream and folded over rose petal preserves. The combination of flavors is quite special, although if you cannot find rose petal preserves (available at Greek and Middle Eastern markets and by mail from Kalustyan), you can substitute cherry preserves with excellent results. Pistachio extract is available from La Cuisine and Dean and Deluca (see list of sources at the end of the book), or substitute 1 teaspoon rose water or vanilla extract.

Dough
- ½ cup milk
- ¼ cup sour cream
- ¼ teaspoon pistachio extract, optional
- 2 large eggs
- 3 tablespoons unsalted butter, cut into small pieces
- ¼ cup sugar
- ½ teaspoon salt
- 2½ cups unbleached white flour
- 2 teaspoons active dry yeast
- ½ cup chopped pistachio nuts

Filling
- ½ cup pistachio nuts
- 1 cup rose petal preserves
- 3 tablespoons unsalted butter, melted, for brushing
  Sugar, for sprinkling

1. Set your bread machine on the dough cycle or equivalent. Add all the dough ingredients, placing them in an order that is appropriate to your model. After the first kneading cycle has finished, turn off the machine and let the dough rise an additional hour in the machine.
2. Meanwhile, prepare the filling. In a food processor fitted with a steel blade, chop the pistachios until powdered. Add the rose petal preserves and pulse to combine.

3. Punch down dough; then remove it to a lightly floured surface. Roll dough out into a 12 × 10–inch rectangle and mark it, lengthwise, into thirds. Cut the outer thirds of the rectangle with a sharp knife about 1 inch apart on an angle. Fill the center third with the rose petal–pistachio filling. Then, starting at the end, fold the strips of cut dough over the filling, crossing them in the center.

4. Transfer the braid to a greased baking tray. Cover with a plastic wrap and let rise in a warm place, until almost doubled in bulk, about 1 hour. Meanwhile, preheat oven to 375 degrees F. Brush loaf with melted butter and sprinkle it generously with sugar. Bake until the top is golden-brown, about 25 minutes.

Serves 6–8

FRESH FRUIT CRUMB CAKE

This fruit-filled crumb cake stays incredibly moist, thanks to the pastry cream in the middle. However, if you haven't the time or inclination to make pastry cream, substitute 1 cup lemon curd, store-bought or homemade (page 166), or try 1 cup sweetened applesauce mixed with 2 tablespoons melted butter and grated nutmeg to taste.

Dough

- 2 large eggs
- ⅓ cup milk
- 4 tablespoons (½ stick) unsalted butter, softened
- 3 tablespoons sugar
- ½ teaspoon grated nutmeg
- ½ teaspoon salt
- 2 cups all-purpose flour
- 1 tablespoon active dry yeast

Streusel

- ¼ cup all-purpose flour
- ¼ cup packed light brown sugar
- 2 tablespoons unsalted butter, cut into small pieces
- 1½ tablespoons ground cinnamon
- 1 recipe pastry cream (page 174)
- 3 cups any fresh fruit, sliced (apples, pears, plums, nectarines, bananas, berries, etc., or a combination)

1. Set your bread machine on the dough cycle or equivalent. Add all the dough ingredients, placing them in an order that is appropriate to your model. After the first kneading cycle has finished, turn off the machine and transfer the dough to a gallon-size plastic bag, and allow it to rest in the refrigerator overnight.

2. Prepare the streusel. Place the flour, brown sugar, butter, and cinnamon in a food processor fitted with a steel blade and pulse just to mix. Do not overprocess; the texture should be crumbly. Refrigerate until needed (overnight is fine).

3. Preheat the oven to 375 degrees F. Remove the dough from the refrigerator and press and/or roll it into a greased 13 × 9–inch baking pan. Spread the pastry cream over the dough, leaving a 1-inch border. Lay the fruit over the pastry cream. Top with the streusel and bake until the top is a light golden brown, about 30 to 40 minutes. Cool slightly on a wire rack before serving.

Serves 6–8

BEE-STING CAKE

This recipe produces a flat galette covered with a caramel-nut topping. It reminds me of a Moravian sugar cake, but gooeyer.

Dough
¾ cup milk
¾ cup (1½ sticks) unsalted butter, softened
½ cup sour cream or plain yogurt
2 large eggs
2 large egg yolks
1 teaspoon pure vanilla extract
¾ cup sugar
½ teaspoon salt
4 cups all-purpose flour
1 tablespoon active dry yeast

Glaze
⅔ cup packed light brown sugar
6 tablespoons (¾ stick) unsalted butter
⅓ cup heavy cream
⅓ cup honey
¼ teaspoon fresh lemon juice
1⅓ cups sliced blanched almonds

1. Set your bread machine on the dough cycle or equivalent. Add all the dough ingredients, placing them in an order that is appropriate to your model.
2. When the cycle is finished, remove dough from the machine and press or roll it into a 12 × 15–inch baking pan. Cover with a damp towel and let rise until doubled, about 40 to 50 minutes.
3. Meanwhile, prepare the glaze. In a small, heavy saucepan, stir together the brown sugar, butter, cream, and honey over medium heat. Bring to a boil, stirring to dissolve the sugar; boil for 30 seconds. Remove pan from the heat and stir in the lemon juice and almonds. Let cool slightly.

4. Preheat the oven to 375 degrees F. Drizzle the warm glaze evenly over the dough. Bake until nuts are golden-brown, about 30 to 35 minutes. Let cool to lukewarm or room temperature in the pan on a wire rack.

Serves 8–10

WINTER SQUASH AND CARAMELIZED APPLE GALETTE

Canned pumpkin puree makes an excellent substitute for the winter squash puree in this recipe, which is really like a cross between a sweet pizza and a tarte tatin. It makes an elegant conclusion to any meal, and the leftovers are terrific for breakfast in the morning.

Dough
 ¾ cup winter squash puree (frozen is okay)
 ¼ cup honey
 5 tablespoons unsalted butter, softened
 1 large egg
 1½ teaspoons salt
 ½ teaspoon ground cinnamon
 ½ teaspoon ground cardamom
 2¾ cups all-purpose flour
 2 teaspoons active dry yeast

Topping
 2 large Granny Smith apples, peeled and thinly sliced
 2 tablespoons unsalted butter
 2 tablespoons packed light brown sugar
 2 tablespoons white wine or water

1. Set your bread machine on the dough cycle or equivalent. Add all the dough ingredients, placing them in an order that is appropriate to your model.
2. Meanwhile, prepare the topping. In a large skillet, melt the butter over medium-high heat. Add the apples and sugar and cook, stirring, until the apples begin to caramelize and the sugar melts, about 5 minutes. Add the wine or water and continue to cook until the liquid is evaporated and the apples are tender, about 3 minutes longer. Remove pan from the heat.
3. When the cycle is finished, remove dough to a lightly floured surface and roll it into a 14-inch circle. Carefully move

the dough to a greased baking sheet. Spoon the apple topping evenly over the dough, leaving a ½-inch border. Cover galette with a damp towel and let rise until doubled, about 45 minutes.
4. Preheat oven to 400 degrees F. Bake galette for 15 to 20 minutes, or until golden-brown and bubbling. Remove it from the oven and let cool slightly on a wire rack. Serve warm or at room temperature.

Serves 6–8

BLACK SESAME COFFEE RING

Black sesame powder is available in Chinese markets, where it is sold to be made into a hot beverage or gruel-like sweet soup. It has a distinctly earthy, nutty flavor that is perfectly balanced by the butter and eggs in the filling. This is an unusual cake that you will either love or hate. I adore it and serve it for breakfast with sliced strawberries and cardamom tea.

Dough
- ¾ cup milk
- 1 large egg
- 2 tablespoons packed dark brown sugar
  Grated zest of 1 lemon
- 4 tablespoons (½ stick) unsalted butter, softened
- ½ teaspoon salt
- 2½ cups all-purpose flour
- 1½ teaspoons yeast

Filling
- ⅔ cup black sesame powder
- 2 large egg yolks
- ¼ cup unsalted butter, softened

Topping
- 2 tablespoons heavy cream
- 2 tablespoons sesame seeds, preferably black
- 1 tablespoon sugar

1. Set your bread machine on the dough cycle or equivalent. Add all the dough ingredients, placing them in an order that is appropriate to your model.
2. Meanwhile, prepare the filling by combining the sesame powder, egg yolks, and butter in the bowl of a food processor fitted with a steel blade. Process the mixture until it is smooth, about 20 seconds.

3. When the cycle is complete, remove the dough from the machine and roll it out to a 12 × 24–inch rectangle. Spread with the filling to within ½ inch of the edges. Starting with a long side, roll up the dough tightly, jelly roll style. Form the roll into a ring, pinching the ends together to seal. Place the ring, seam side down, onto a greased baking sheet. Cover the loaf with plastic wrap and let rise until almost doubled, about 45 minutes.

4. Preheat the oven to 375 degrees F. Brush top of the loaf with the heavy cream, then sprinkle on the sesame seeds and sugar. Bake loaf for about 20 to 25 minutes, or until the top is golden-brown. Remove tray to a wire rack to cool slightly.

Serves 6

SWEET CHESTNUT AND RUM
COFFEE LOG

The sweetened chestnut puree (*creme de marrons* in French—it is frequently imported) gives this loaf its sweet and toasty character. Look for it in large supermarkets and gourmet specialty stores. You can also order it from Williams-Sonoma, Kalustyan, or Dean and Deluca (see the list of sources at the end of the book)

Dough
- ¾ **cup milk**
- 4 **tablespoons (½ stick) unsalted butter**
- 1 **tablespoon dark rum**
- ⅓ **cup sweetened chestnut puree**
- 4 **tablespoons packed dark brown sugar**
- ½ **teaspoon salt**
- 2⅔ **cups all-purpose flour**
- 1½ **teaspoons active dry yeast**

Filling
- 2 **tablespoons unsalted butter, melted**
- ⅓ **cup sweetened chestnut puree**
- 2 **tablespoons dark rum**

Glaze
- 2 **tablespoons heavy cream**

1. Set your bread machine on the dough cycle or equivalent. Add all the dough ingredients, placing them in an order that is appropriate to your model.
2. When the cycle is complete, remove the dough from the machine and roll it out to a 10 × 15–inch rectangle. Brush with the melted butter and spread with the chestnut puree to within ½ inch of the edges; drizzle with the rum.
3. Starting with a short side, roll up the dough tightly, jelly-roll style. Transfer the log to a greased baking sheet and brush

with the glaze. Cover the ring with plastic wrap and let rise until almost doubled, about 45 minutes.

4. Preheat the oven to 375 degrees F. Bake ring for about 25 minutes, or until the top is golden-brown. Remove tray to a wire rack to cool slightly.

Serves 8

MANGO CREAM SHORTCAKES

Juicy, lush mangoes usually need no accompaniment other than a sink to eat them over. However, there are those rare times when something more fussy is desired. This recipe fits the bill, since it leaves the cubes of mango untouched and finds embellishment in the accoutrements.

Dough
  1 large egg
  ¾ cup buttermilk
  4 tablespoons (½ stick) unsalted butter, cut into pieces
  ⅓ cup plus 2 tablespoons sugar
  ½ teaspoon allspice
  ½ teaspoon salt
  2½ cups plus 2 tablespoons all-purpose flour
  1½ teaspoons active dry yeast
  ¼ cup chopped dried mango

Topping
  4 ripe mangoes, peeled and cubed
  1⅓ cups heavy cream
  2 tablespoons confectioners' sugar, if desired
  2 tablespoons lime juice

1. Set your bread machine on the dough cycle or equivalent. Add all the dough ingredients, placing them in an order that is appropriate to your model. After letting the machine knead the ingredients for 3 to 5 minutes, when the dough has come together and looks like a cross between a dough and a batter, turn off the bread machine. Allow the dough to rise in the machine for 45 minutes.

2. Punch down dough and remove it to a lightly floured work surface. Roll it into a 7 × 5-inch rectangle. The dough should be about 1 inch thick. Using a 2-inch round cutter, cut out 6 biscuits. Place them, two inches apart, on a greased baking

tray. Cover biscuits with a clean towel and let rise for 15 minutes.

3. Preheat oven to 400 degrees F. Brush the biscuits with the melted butter and bake until they are golden brown, about 15 to 18 minutes. Remove baking tray to a wire rack and let the biscuits cool completely.

4. Meanwhile, whip the cream until it begins to thicken. Add the sugar and lime juice and continue whipping until it holds soft peaks. To serve, cut the biscuits in half crosswise and arrange the bottoms on serving plates. Top with some of the whipped cream, then with some of the mango cubes. Replace biscuit tops. Serve shortcakes with more whipped cream and mangoes around the plate.

Serves 6

KOUGIN AMANN

This wonderfully flaky French pastry (pronounced *kween aman*) is a specialty of Brittany, where it is served as a snack with coffee.

1½ **tablespoons active dry yeast**
1 **teaspoon salt**
2 **cups all-purpose flour**
11 **tablespoons unsalted butter (keep 8 tablespoons in refrigerator until ready to use)**
1¼ **cups sugar**

1. Set your bread machine on the dough cycle or equivalent. Add all the dough ingredients, placing them in an order that is appropriate to your model. After about 12 minutes of the first kneading (the dough should look smooth and elastic), turn the machine off and let the dough rise in the pan until almost doubled in bulk, about 1 hour.
2. Remove dough from the machine. Roll out dough on a lightly floured surface into a large rectangle, about 12 × 18 inches, with the shorter side nearest you.
3. Cut chilled stick of butter into 10 to 12 pieces. Dot middle third of dough with butter pieces and sprinkle with ¾ cup of sugar. Working quickly, fold short sides toward the center, over the butter and sugar. Edges should slightly overlap. Sprinkle dough with sugar, and roll over seams to seal. Turn dough again, so that the shorter side is nearest you, and fold into thirds, as you would a letter. Let dough rest 15 minutes in refrigerator.
4. Preheat oven to 450 degrees F. Grease a 9-inch pie pan with butter and dust with flour. Sprinkle work surface with sugar. Roll out dough, dusting with ¼ cup sugar as you go, into a large rectangle. Fold into thirds again and let dough rest another 15 minutes in refrigerator.
5. Again sprinkle work surface with sugar. Roll out dough, dusting with remaining ¼ cup sugar as you go, into a rough

round, slightly larger than pie pan. Ease dough into pan. Melt remaining 3 tablespoons butter and drizzle over dough. Sprinkle with any sugar swept up from the work surface, and bake until golden, 35 to 40 minutes. Remove from pan while hot and serve warm.

Serves 6–8

SAVARIN

A savarin is essentially a brioche that is baked into a ring shape and then soaked in a kirsch-flavored sugar syrup. It is usually served with whipped cream and fruit, although it is also quite nice just plain, when its buttery, eggy flavor and moist texture aren't at all overshadowed.

Dough
- 3 large eggs
- 3 tablespoons water
- 3 tablespoons sugar
- ½ teaspoon salt
- 2 cups all-purpose flour
- 1½ teaspoons active dry yeast
- ¾ cup (1½ sticks) unsalted butter, cut into small pieces

Syrup
- 2 cups water
- 1 cup sugar
- ¾ to 1 cup kirsch

Glaze
- ½ to ¾ cup apricot jam
- 1 teaspoon kirsch

1. Place the all the dough ingredients except the butter in the bread machine in an order appropriate to your model. Leave the butter in a warm place to soften while the bread is kneading.
2. When the dough is done with its first rising (this will be at different times in different machines but will generally be about halfway through the cycle), remove the dough from the machine (do not turn it off) and place it with the softened butter in the bowl of a food processor. Pulse the processor on and off until the butter is just incorporated into the dough. This should take about 15 to 30 seconds. Do not overprocess

the dough; it doesn't matter if the dough is completely smooth, as long as no large chunks of butter remain visible. If using an electric mixer, mix together the dough and butter at medium speed for about 45 seconds to 1 minute. A food processor is better than a mixer since it works the butter into the dough faster.

3. Savarin is traditionally baked in a ring mold, but I like to use a Bundt pan or even a 9-inch springform pan. Fill whichever pan (greased) half full. Let rise in a warm place again until the dough just reaches the top of the pan, about 1 hour.

4. Meanwhile, preheat oven to 350 degrees F. Bake savarin for 55 minutes to 1 hour, or until it is firm, golden-brown, and pulling away from the sides.

5. While the cake is baking, make the syrup. Boil the water and sugar together for a few minutes, stirring to dissolve the sugar, then remove from the heat and let cool slightly. Stir in the kirsch. When the cake comes from the oven, prick the top with a fork and turn out onto a baking sheet—one with sides, not a flat one. Spoon the syrup over the savarin gradually while it is still warm and let it stand to soak up the syrup from the bottom of the pan, spooning some over the top occasionally.

6. When the syrup has been absorbed, heat the apricot jam, stirring, until it is smooth and hot. Brush the cake with the jam, reheating as necessary. Move the cake carefully to a serving plate. When you are ready to serve it, heat the jam again and brush on a final coat to make the cake shine.

Serves 8

RUM BABAS

Babas are savarins that are soaked in a rum-flavored, rather than kirsch-flavored, syrup and are usually baked in small, round molds, or, as in this case, muffin tins. You can split them and fill then with pastry cream (page 174), lemon curd (page 166), or bourbon cream (page 178), substituting rum for the bourbon.

If you haven't soaked your raisins overnight, you can heat them with rum to cover in a small saucepan until they simmer. Remove pan from the heat and let sit for 15 minutes before proceeding with the recipe.

Dough
   3 large eggs
   2 tablespoons water
   2 tablespoons honey
   ½ teaspoon salt
   2 cups all-purpose flour
   1½ teaspoons active dry yeast
   ¾ cup (1½ sticks) unsalted butter, cut into small pieces
   ½ cup golden raisins, soaked overnight in rum

Syrup
   2 cups water
   1 cup sugar
   ¾ to 1 cup rum

1. Place the all the dough ingredients except the butter and raisins in the bread machine in an order appropriate to your model. Leave the butter in a warm place to soften while the bread is kneading.
2. When the dough is done with its first rising (this will be at different times in different machines but will generally be about halfway through the cycle), remove the dough from the machine (do not turn it off) and place it with the softened butter in the bowl of a food processor. Pulse the processor on

and off until the butter is just incorporated into the dough. This should take about 15 to 30 seconds. Do not overprocess the dough; it doesn't matter if the dough is completely smooth, as long as no large chunks of butter remain visible. If using an electric mixer, mix together the dough and butter at medium speed for about 45 seconds to 1 minute. A food processor is better than a mixer since it works the butter into the dough faster.

3. Fill greased baba molds or muffin tins half-full with the dough; then let rise until doubled, about 35 minutes.

4. Meanwhile, preheat oven to 350 degrees F. Bake until the babas are golden-brown and firm, about 15 to 20 minutes.

5. While the babas are baking, make the syrup. Boil the water and sugar together for a few minutes, stirring to dissolve the sugar. Remove pan from the heat and let cool slightly. Stir in the rum. When the babas come out of the oven, prick the tops with a fork and turn out onto a baking sheet—one with sides, not a flat one. Ladle the syrup over the babas gradually while they are still warm, and let them stand to soak up the syrup from the bottom of the pan, spooning some over the tops occasionally.

Serves 12

DESSERT PIZZAS, CALZONES, AND FOCACCIA

RICE PUDDING CALZONE

As an incorrigible rice pudding lover, I am always on the look-out for an excuse to whip up a batch. With this recipe, not only do I get to enjoy my pudding wrapped in chewy pastry, I also get to eat the leftover pudding, straight up with a spoon.

Dough
½ cup milk
 4 tablespoons (½ stick) unsalted butter
 2 large eggs
 1 teaspoon balsamic vinegar
½ cup sugar
½ teaspoon salt
½ cup semolina flour
 2 cups all-purpose flour
 1 tablespoon active dry yeast

Filling
 2 cups homemade (page 170) or purchased rice pudding

1. Set your bread machine on the dough cycle or equivalent. Add all the dough ingredients, placing them in an order appropriate to your model. At the end of the second kneading cycle, turn the machine off and let the dough rise in the machine for 30 minutes. Transfer the dough to a plastic bag and refrigerate it for 1½ hours.
2. Preheat oven to 375 degrees F. Remove the dough from the refrigerator, divide it in half, and roll each half out on a lightly floured surface into a 14-inch circle. Cover with a kitchen towel and let rest for 10 minutes. Place half the filling in the center of each circle and fold it in half. Twist the seams closed.
3. Place the calzones on greased baking sheets, cover with kitchen towels, and let them rise for 20 minutes. Bake them in the oven for 20 to 25 minutes, or until they are light brown. Serve slightly warm or at room temperature.

Serves 8

COFFEE CREAM CALZONE WITH CHOCOLATE CHIPS

This is always a big hit, especially with the tiramisu-loving crowd.

Dough
- ½ cup milk
- 4 tablespoons (½ stick) unsalted butter, softened
- 2 large eggs
- 1 teaspoon salt
- ⅓ cup sugar
- 2½ cups all-purpose flour
- 2½ teaspoons active dry yeast

Filling
- 2 teaspoons instant coffee powder
- 2 tablespoons hot kalhua or brandy
- 1 cup ricotta cheese
- 1 large egg
- ⅓ cup sugar
- ¾ cup chocolate chips

1. Set your bread machine on the dough cycle or equivalent. Add all the dough ingredients, placing them in an order appropriate to your model. At the end of the second kneading cycle, turn the machine off and let the dough rise in the machine for 30 minutes. Transfer the dough to plastic bag and refrigerate it for 1½ hours.

2. While the dough is chilling, make the filling. In a medium bowl, dissolve the coffee powder in the hot kalhua or brandy. Add the ricotta, egg, and sugar and mix very well to combine. Stir in the chocolate chips. Set filling aside (it can be refrigerated for up to 3 days).

3. Preheat oven to 375 degrees F. Remove the dough from the refrigerator, divide it in half, and roll each half out on a lightly floured surface into a 14-inch circle. Cover with a

kitchen towel and let rest for 10 minutes. Place half the filling in the center of each circle and fold it in half. Twist the seams closed.

4. Place the calzones on greased baking sheets, cover with kitchen towels, and let them rise for 20 minutes. Bake them in the oven for 20 to 25 minutes, or until they are light brown. Serve slightly warm or at room temperature.

Serves 8

SWEET ALMOND AND RICOTTA PIZZA

This fun dessert resembles a sweet version of pizza bianca, the kind made only with ricotta and mozzarella cheeses, without tomato sauce. In my dessert version I keep the ricotta and substitute grated almond paste for the mozzarella.

For this recipe, it's best to use the firm almond paste sold in a tube since it grates more easily than the soft kind, which must be frozen first. You could also use marzipan.

Dough
⅓ cup sour cream
1 large egg
1 tablespoon fresh lemon juice
3 tablespoons sugar
½ teaspoon ground mace
½ teaspoon salt
1½ cups all-purpose flour
1½ teaspoons active dry yeast

Topping
1 container (15 ounces) ricotta cheese
¼ cup confectioners' sugar
1 teaspoon grated lemon zest
¼ teaspoon almond extract
3 tablespoons apricot jam
3½ ounces (½ tube) almond paste, grated

1. Set your bread machine on the dough cycle or equivalent. Add all the dough ingredients, placing them in an order appropriate to you model. At the end of the cycle, remove dough from the machine and let it rest for 10 minutes, covered with a kitchen towel.
2. Preheat the oven to 375 degrees F. Grease a 12-inch pizza pan. In a small bowl, combine the ricotta cheese, sugar, lemon zest, and almond extract, mixing well. Reserve.

3. On a lightly floured surface, roll the dough into a 12-inch circle and lift and stretch it into the prepared pan. Spread the apricot jam evenly over the crust. Then spread on the ricotta mixture. Top with grated almond paste. Bake until the crust is golden brown, about 15 to 20 minutes. Remove pizza pan to a wire rack to cool slightly. Serve warm.

Serves 6

FRESH GRAPE SCHIACCIATA

Fresh red grapes make this flat sweet bread explode with their juiciness.

Dough

1 cup warm water
2 tablespoons sugar
3 tablespoons extra virgin olive oil
⅛ teaspoon salt
2⅔ cups all-purpose flour
2 teaspoons active dry yeast

Filling

2 tablespoons extra virgin olive oil
2½ pounds seedless red grapes, stemmed, washed and dried
4 tablespoons sugar
1 large egg, beaten

1. Set your bread machine on the dough cycle or equivalent. Add all the dough ingredients, placing them in an order appropriate to you model. At the end of the cycle, remove dough from the machine and let it rest for 20 minutes, covered with a kitchen towel.
2. Meanwhile, preheat the oven to 375 degrees F. Place the dough onto a floured surface and roll it into a 16 × 20–inch rectangle. Place the dough into a greased 15 × 18–inch baking pan, letting the edges hang over the sides of the pan. Brush the dough with the olive oil, then scatter the grapes evenly over the top. Sprinkle 2 tablespoons of the sugar evenly over the grapes.
3. Bring the overhanging dough from the 2 longest sides toward the middle and pinch the seam together. Cut most of the excess dough off the 2 remaining short sides, leaving about ½ inch extending. Then fold the dough in on itself, pinching the ends closed.

4. Reroll the scraps of dough into a rectangle and cut it into ½-inch strips. Use the strips to make a crisscross pattern over the grapes. Gently brush the top all over with the beaten egg and sprinkle with the remaining 2 tablespoons of sugar. Bake on the middle rack for 30 to 35 minutes, or until the dough is golden-brown on top and browned on the bottom.

5. Remove pan to a wire rack to cool for at least 30 minutes before serving. Serve that same day.

Serves 8–10

SWEET LAVENDER FOCACCIA

Flavored with orange zest and lavender, this lightly sweet, airy bread is perfect for breakfast when something less rich is desired.

Crushing the lavender flowers before adding them to the dough helps release their piney flavor. If you are not a lavender fan, or cannot procure it, substitute 1 teaspoon ground cinnamon or 1 teaspoon fennel seeds.

Dough
¾ cup water
1 large egg
2 tablespoons unsalted butter, melted
¼ cup sugar
  Grated zest or one orange
1 teaspoon dried lavender flowers, crushed and bruised with the side of a knife
1 tablespoon pure vanilla extract
2 cups unbleached all-purpose flour
1 tablespoon active dry yeast

Topping
2 tablespoons unsalted butter, melted
  Confectioners' sugar, for sprinkling

1. Set your bread machine on the dough cycle or equivalent. Add all the dough ingredients, placing them in an order appropriate to your model. At the end of the cycle, remove dough from the machine, pour and scrape it (the dough will be soft and batterlike) into a greased 9 × 13–inch baking pan.
2. Brush the melted butter over the top of the dough; let rise in a warm spot for about 1½ hours.
3. Preheat the oven to 325 degrees F. Bake the focaccia for 15 to 20 minutes, or until the top is nicely browned. Remove pan to a wire rack and let cool completely. Before serving, cut focaccia into squares and dust with confectioner's sugar.

Serves 8

TRIFLES, BREAD PUDDINGS, SWEET SANDWICHES, AND OTHER DESSERTS USING BREADS FROM THE MACHINE

CHESTNUT HONEY BRIOCHE
BREAD PUDDING

Stale brioche (or other bread) works best in most bread pudding recipes since the dry cubes can absorb custard more thirstily than fresh. However, if you only have a fresh brioche nearby, cut it into cubes and toast it in a 300 degree F oven until it feels dry, about 20 minutes. You can substitute any other type of brioche for the chestnut honey loaf in this recipe. Pistachio and prune-Armagnac are also wonderful.

- 1 **loaf stale chestnut honey brioche (p. 53), cut into cubes**
- 2 **cups whole milk**
- ½ **cup raisins**
- 2 **tablespoons unsalted butter, melted**
- ½ **cup sugar**
- 2 **large egg yolks**
- 1 **large egg**
- 1 **tablespoon pure vanilla extract**
- ¼ **teaspoon freshly grated nutmeg**
- 2 **tablespoons fresh lemon juice**

1. Preheat the oven to 350 degrees F. Butter a 1-quart shallow baking dish.
2. In large bowl, combine the brioche cubes, raisins, and milk. In another bowl, whisk together the sugar, egg yolks, egg, lemon juice, vanilla, and nutmeg until very smooth. Add the egg mixture to the bread mixture and stir to combine. Let the mixture rest for at least 15 minutes at room temperature, or for up to 1 hour, refrigerated.
3. Pour the pudding mixture into the prepared baking dish. Bake until the pudding is firm and a knife inserted into the middle emerges clean, about 35 minutes. Cool to room temperature on a wire rack.

Serves 6–8

SAINT LOUIS GOOEY CAKE

You really can use almost any type of coffee cake for this aptly named confection. Or combine the remains of several loaves if you happen to have them. I like to freeze stray slices of leftover cake, letting them collect in a plastic bag, until there is enough to make this recipe. I love the element of nostalgia as I bite into the reincarnated remnants of loaves-gone-by.

1 recipe any coffee cake (or a combination), cut into ½-inch slices (about 4 cups)
½ cup (1 stick) unsalted butter, softened
1¼ cups sugar
  Pinch salt
1 large egg
2 tablespoons light corn syrup
2 tablespoons water
2 teaspoons pure vanilla extract
1 cup all-purpose flour
  Confectioners' sugar, for sprinkling

1. Butter a 9-inch pan. Cut the coffee cake into wedges or rectangles. Fit the cake into the pan, pressing and molding the slices together to form a single layer.
2. In a large bowl with an electric mixer on medium-high speed, beat the butter, sugar, and salt until very smooth. Add the egg and beat well. Beat in the corn syrup, water, and vanilla until smooth. Reduce speed to low and mix in the flour.
3. Punch holes in the coffee cake with a fork. Pour the batter all over the cake. Let stand for 20 minutes. Meanwhile, preheat the oven to 375 degrees F.
4. Bake until the top of the cake is bubbling and golden, about 30 minutes; do not overbake (the topping will not be gooey if baked too long). Cool the cake in the pan on a wire rack. Sprinkle with confectioners' sugar before serving.

Serves 8

QUINCE, ORANGE, AND PISTACHIO CHARLOTTE

Every autumn for the past several years, my family has been given a bushel of quinces as a gift from a quince tree owner. And every year we agonize over how to use them up. Since quinces cannot be eaten out of hand and demand not only cooking but sweetening as well, they tend to lend themselves to more elaborate preparations, like this lovely charlotte. But there are only so many elaborate preparations one family can construct and consume before the quinces decompose in the back of the fridge. So no matter how many quince things we made—quince bread, quince sorbet, quince cheese, quince tart, quince custard, quince sauce—there were still quinces left over (they must have multiplied like bunnies in the refrigerator crisper). However, they always made the refrigerator smell wonderful, even when they turned to liquid.

If you don't have quinces to use up, you can substitute Granny Smith apples. You can also substitute maple-oat or chestnut honey brioche for the pistachio, or try the butterscotch pear bread on page 47.

¾ cup (1-½ sticks) melted butter, divided
5 medium quinces, peeled, cored and cut into 1-inch cubes
2 tablespoons orange juice
⅓ cup sugar
½ teaspoon allspice
   Grated zest of one small orange
1 loaf pistachio brioche, sliced
1 12-ounce jar orange marmalade
½ cup chopped pistachio nuts
5 tablespoons Grand Marnier, Cointreau, or brandy (or substitute orange juice)
   Whipped cream, for serving

1. Heat 2 tablespoons of the melted butter in a large skillet or saucepan over medium heat. Add the quinces and toss to coat them with butter. Add the orange juice and cook the mixture, stirring occasionally, until the fruit is very tender, about 10 minutes. Add the sugar, allspice, and orange zest and cook, stirring, until the sugar dissolves. Remove the pan from the heat.

2. If you have one, dig out a 1½–quart charlotte mold or deep souffle dish. If you don't, substitute a deep (at least 3 inches) 9-inch round cake pan. In a pinch, use a deep, ovenproof bowl. Using the mold or baking dish as your guide, cut 6 slices of the brioche into triangles and then cut the remaining slices into long, thin rectangles. Dip one side of half the bread triangles in the remaining melted butter and arrange them, side by side, buttered side down, and points to the center, over the bottom of the mold. Repeat process for the sides of the mold using the rectangles, overlapping them slightly. The point is to cover the bottom and sides of the mold as tightly as possible with the brioche. Don't worry if your attempt is a bit messy. Reserve the remaining brioche triangles for the top.

3. Preheat the oven to 400 degrees F. Place half of the quince mixture in the brioche-lined mold, pressing the brioche down against the mold. Add about a third of the marmalade, then sprinkle on half the pistachio nuts, and a tablespoon of the liqueur. Add the remaining fruit, another third of marmalade, and another tablespoon or so of the liqueur. Dip one side of the remaining bread triangles in the remaining butter, arrange on top of the mold, buttered sides up, points in, and sprinkle the bread with another tablespoon of liqueur.

4. Set the mold on a baking sheet, place in the oven, and immediately lower the temperature to 375 degrees. Bake for 35 minutes. If after 15 or 20 minutes the pieces of brioche on the top are browning too quickly, cover the mold loosely with buttered foil.

5. Meanwhile, in a small saucepan, melt the remaining marmalade over low heat. Strain and stir in the remaining brandy. Strain into a small bowl.

6. When the top of the charlotte is golden-brown, remove to a wire rack. Let cool for 10 to 15 minutes. Gently invert the charlotte onto a serving platter and let it cool for about 10 minutes longer. Carefully remove the mold, and brush the charlotte with the warm strained marmalade. Serve immediately, with the whipped cream on the side, if desired.

Serves 6–8

SUMMER PUDDING

I like to use the startling colored blue bread (page 51) for this ripe dessert, which is only a pudding in the sense that the British call any type of dessert a "pudding." It is really a fresh berry torte.

Make sure your bread is stale (or at least dried out in a low oven). Otherwise the pudding is apt to fall apart soggily.

2½ cups fresh, ripe summer berries (use a combination
    such as blackberries, red currants, raspberries,
    blueberries, and/or strawberries, and quarter the
    strawberries if large)
½ cup sugar, or to taste (more if you use red currants)
2 tablespoons cold water
1 loaf stale blue bread (page 51) or brioche, preferably
    cornmeal or chestnut honey, cut into ½-inch slices
    Whipped cream, heavy cream, or vanilla frozen
    yogurt for serving

1. In a medium saucepan, stir together the berries, sugar, and water. Cover and bring to a simmer. Uncover the pan, reduce heat to very low, and gently stir the mixture, taking care not to mash the berries, until the sugar is dissolved, about 1 or 2 minutes. Remove the pan from the heat. Taste and add more sugar if needed.

2. Line the bottom and sides of a deep 8-inch cake pan or 1-quart mold with ¾ of the bread, cutting the slices to fit together snugly. The mold should be completely lined with bread. Set the mold and the remaining bread aside.

3. With a slotted spoon, spoon the berries into the bread-lined mold. Spoon some of the juice, but not all, over the fruit; reserve the remaining juice. Strain the remaining juice and add the solids to the mold. Cover and refrigerate the reserved juice.

4. Cover the berries in the bowl with a neat, flat layer of bread triangles, points toward the center. Patch any open spaces carefully with bread scraps. Invert a plate that is slightly smaller

than the mold directly on the bread inside the rim. Place the mold on a baking sheet to catch any drips. Weigh down the plate with a heavy can or other weight; refrigerate the pudding overnight. After several hours, check to see if any parts of the bread are still dry; if so, spoon a little of the reserved berry juice over them so that all parts of the bread are soaked with juice.

5. To serve, remove the weight and plate. Run the tip of a knife all around the sides of the mold, and invert the pudding onto a serving plate. Serve with whipped cream, heavy cream, or frozen yogurt on the side.

Serves 8

BANANA CAPRIOTADA

This is a banana version of the typically apple Spanish-inspired bread pudding. You can substitute any other type of sweet bread for the banana bread and chopped apples for the bananas if you want to be more traditional.

While the bread for this recipe doesn't have to be stale, it works best if it is a day old.

½ cup (1 stick) unsalted butter
½ loaf day-old banana bread with malted milk
  (page 46), cut into 1-inch cubes
1 pound (1 box) dark brown sugar
1½ cups water
1½ teaspoons ground cinnamon
2 medium ripe bananas, peeled and sliced
1 cup walnuts, chopped
½ pound cream cheese, chilled and chopped
  Heavy cream for garnish

1. Preheat oven to 350 degrees F. Butter a 13 × 9–inch pan.
2. Melt the butter in a medium saucepan, and add the bread cubes and stir to coat evenly. Spread the cubes on a baking sheet and bake until they are lightly brown and crisp, about 15 minutes. Remove the bread and raise the oven temperature to 400 degrees.
3. Combine the brown sugar and water in a saucepan over medium-high heat and bring to a boil, stirring. Remove pan from the heat and stir in the cinnamon.
4. In a large mixing bowl, combine the bananas, walnuts, cream cheese, and toasted bread cubes. Drizzle with the brown sugar syrup and mix to evenly distribute. Transfer the mixture to the prepared pan.
5. Bake, uncovered, stirring occasionally, for 15 minutes.

Then bake for an additional 10 to 15 minutes, without stirring, until the top is golden-brown and crusty and the liquid is almost gone. Serve warm with heavy cream.

Serves 8

PAIN PERDUE SOUFFLÉ

If you didn't soak the raisins overnight, you can place them in a small saucepan with rum to cover, bring to a simmer, and then turn off the heat and let the raisins steep for 15 minutes before using.

 3 cups chopped Danish pastry or croissant
½ cup heavy cream
 6 large eggs, separated
¼ cup sugar, plus additional for coating the dish
¼ cup raisins, soaked overnight in rum and drained
 1 teaspoon pure vanilla extract
½ cup confectioners' sugar, plus additional for serving

1. Preheat the oven to 375 degrees. Butter a 1½–quart soufflé dish and coat it with sugar. In a large bowl, combine the chopped Danish pastry or croissant with the heavy cream, tossing to combine. Let mixture sit while preparing the remaining ingredients.

2. Place the egg yolks and sugar in the top of a double boiler or in a stainless steel bowl suspended over simmering water. Whisk mixture until frothy and the sugar has dissolved, about 3 to 4 minutes. Remove top from over water.

3. Add the egg yolk mixture to the pastry mixture and mix well, making sure the bread is well coated with the egg. Stir in the raisins and vanilla. In another large bowl, beat the egg whites until frothy. Gradually add the confectioners' sugar and beat until the egg whites form stiff peaks. Gently fold the beaten egg whites into the pudding mixture. Transfer soufflé mixture to the prepared baking pan.

4. Bake until the soufflé is lightly golden-brown and set, but still slightly wobbly in the center, about 35 to 40 minutes. Sprinkle the soufflé with additional confectioners' sugar and serve immediately.

Serves 6–8

CHOCOLATE CORNMEAL BREAD PUDDING WITH BOURBON CREAM

Use your favorite eating bittersweet chocolate for this recipe, and it will become your favorite bread pudding, too.

8 ounces bittersweet chocolate, finely chopped
4 tablespoons (½ stick) unsalted butter
3 cups whole milk
1 cup heavy cream
1 cup sugar
6 large egg yolks
2 tablespoons bourbon
  Pinch salt
1 loaf stale cornmeal brioche, cut into 12 slices
1 recipe bourbon cream (page 178)

1. Preheat oven to 425 degrees F. Suspend the top of a double boiler or a stainless steel bowl over hot, not simmering, water. Add the chocolate and butter and stir until the mixture is melted and smooth. Remove bowl from over water.
2. Heat the cream and milk in a saucepan and bring to a bare simmer. Meanwhile, whisk the sugar and yolks in a large bowl until well blended. Slowly whisk in the cream-and-milk mixture. Add the yolk mixture to the melted chocolate, whisking constantly. Stir in the bourbon and salt.
3. In a 9 × 12–inch baking dish, arrange the brioche in 2 overlapping rows. Pour the chocolate mixture over the brioche, cover with plastic wrap, and place a smaller pan on top of the brioche so that the slices stay submerged. Weight the top with cans if necessary.
4. Let stand for 1 hour or until bread is soaked through. Preheat oven to 325 degrees F. Remove the weights, pan, and plastic wrap, and cover pan with foil. Punch with holes to

allow steam to escape. Bake pudding until the liquid has been absorbed and pudding has a glossy look, about 1 hour. Serve warm, with the bourbon cream.

Serves 6

CHOCOLATE CRUMB BAVARIAN

I like to make this puddinglike, molded dessert with chocolate bread crumbs from the chocolate brioche on page 65. However, you really can use any crumbs, including those from plain, nonsweet loaves; the recipe it is based on called for pumpernickel. If raspberry sauce doesn't entice you as a companion for this creamy dessert, substitute chocolate sauce (page 179), or caramel sauce (page 176).

2½ cups fine sweet bread crumbs (any will do)
2 cups whole milk
½ cup sugar
2 tablespoons kirsch or brandy
1 envelope powdered gelatin
3 large egg yolks, lightly beaten
1 teaspoon pure vanilla extract
½ cup heavy cream, stiffly whipped
1 recipe raspberry sauce, page 182
1 pint fresh raspberries

1. Place the crumbs in a large heatproof bowl. Bring 1 cup of the milk and ¼ cup of the sugar to a boil in a small heavy saucepan over moderate heat. Pour over the crumbs, add the kirsch or brandy and mix well. Cover the bread crumb mixture and let stand 2 hours at room temperature.

2. In a small heavy saucepan (you can use the same one), combine the remaining milk and remaining sugar. Sprinkle in the gelatin and let mixture stand for 5 minutes. Turn the heat on to low and cook, stirring often, just until the gelatin and sugar dissolve, about 5 minutes. Whisk a little of the hot milk mixture into the beaten yolks to temper them, then stir the warmed yolks back into the pan, and cook, stirring constantly, over low heat for about 5 minutes. You are looking for a very thin custard that will just coat the back of a spoon.

3. Remove the custard from the heat and stir in the vanilla. Place the pan with the custard in a large bowl or sink filled

with ice water and chill the mixture, whisking briskly, until it is cool to the touch. Blend the cooled custard into the crumb mixture, then fold in the whipped cream. Ladle into 6 ramekins, cover each with plastic wrap, and chill for at least 8 hours or overnight.

4. To serve, run the tip of a sharp knife around the bavarians and unmold them onto serving plates. Serve with raspberry sauce and raspberries, if desired.

Serves 6

SOUR CHERRY TRIFLE

For a chocolate version of this trifle, make it with the chocolate chip butterscotch pudding cake on page 98, or chocolate brioche (page 65). As for the sour cherries, I like to use the water-packed kind sold in a glass jar, usually imported from Eastern Europe, although canned sour cherries will also do. Do not use canned sour cherry pie filling, which is much too gloppy and fruit-sparse.

½ loaf any sweet bread or cake
3 tablespoons unsalted butter, melted
2 tablespoons cream sherry
2 tablespoons dark rum
1 cup water-packed sour cherries (drain before measuring)
½ cup best-quality sour cherry or apricot jam
2 cups crème Anglaise (page 173)
1 cup cold heavy cream
2 teaspoons confectioners' sugar
½ teaspoon pure vanilla extract
⅓ cup slivered almonds, for garnish

1. Preheat broiler. Cut the sweet bread into thick slices and brush them with butter on one side. Lay the slices on a baking sheet, butter-side up, and toast them under the broiler until they are pale golden-brown. Remove baking tray and let cool slightly. Fit the bread into the bottom of a decorative 1½–quart glass bowl, making a fairly solid layer. Sprinkle the sherry and rum over the bread.
2. In a bowl, mix the cherries (reserving a few for decoration) with the jam. Spread the cherry mixture evenly over the bread, making sure the cherries reach the edges of the bowl so they are visible. Pour the crème Anglaise over the cherries. Cover the bowl with plastic wrap and refrigerate for 2 hours or longer to allow the ingredients to soak together and combine their flavors.

3. A bit before serving, whip the cream with the confectioners' sugar and vanilla until thick. Spread the cream over the trifle. Decorate the top with reserved cherries and sprinkle the almonds over the top and serve, spooning up the trifle from the bottom to include the bread in each serving.

Serves 6

CLASSIC BOSTOCK

Bostock is a treat that bakers in France make with their left-over brioche. They dip day-old slices into a kirsch-flavored sugar syrup; then cover them with almond cream before baking. The result is like an almond croissant, only more cakelike and firmer. Traditionally, bostock is eaten out of hand as a snack with coffee or tea, or even as breakfast, but given its richness, I prefer to serve it for dessert, with lightly sweetened whipped cream and raspberry sauce (page 182).

1 loaf any brioche, cut into 10 slices
1¼ cups slivered blanched almonds
1 cup water
1½ cups sugar
3 tablespoons kirsch or brandy
2 large eggs

1. Preheat the oven to 375 degrees F. Toast the almonds on a baking sheet until lightly browned, about 5 minutes. Remove baking tray, but leave the oven on. When the almonds have cooled, grind ¾ cup of them to a fine powder in a food processor. Coarsely chop the remaining almonds.

2. In a medium-size saucepan over medium-high heat, combine the water and ⅔ cup sugar and cook, stirring, until the sugar is dissolved and the syrup thickens slightly, about 5 minutes. Remove the syrup from the heat and stir in the kirsch.

3. Dip the slices of brioche in the syrup and drain them on a wire rack. Once drained, arrange the slices on a buttered baking sheet.

4. In a small mixing bowl combine the eggs, finely ground almonds, and remaining sugar and blend to a thick paste. Spread the mixture on the brioche, then sprinkle with the coarsely chopped almonds. Bake for 15 minutes or until golden-brown. Serve warm for dessert, or at room temperature for a snack.

Serves 10

MAPLE-WALNUT BOSTOCK

This is my American version of a classic French preparation for using up day-old brioche (see page 57 for the classic version). Instead of preparing a sugar syrup, as called for in the original recipe, I have substituted maple syrup, which cuts out a step and adds a delicious, toasty flavor. Walnuts replace almonds, and dark rum replaces kirsch. Serve this warm for dessert, with an appropriate ice cream and fresh fruit.

- 1 loaf any brioche, preferably maple-oat, cut into 10 slices
- 1¼ cups walnuts
- 1½ cups pure maple syrup
- ¾ cup maple or packed light brown sugar
- 3 tablespoons dark rum
- 2 large eggs

1. Preheat the oven to 375 degrees F. Toast the walnuts on a baking sheet until lightly browned and fragrant, about 8 minutes. Remove baking tray, but leave the oven on. When the nuts have cooled, grind ¾ cup of them to a fine powder in a food processor. Coarsely chop the remaining walnuts.
2. In a medium bowl, combine the maple syrup and rum. Dip the slices of brioche in the syrup and drain them on a wire rack. Once drained, arrange the slices on a buttered baking sheet.
3. In a small mixing bowl combine the eggs, finely ground walnuts, and sugar and blend to a thick paste. Spread the mixture on the brioche, then sprinkle with the coarsely chopped walnuts. Bake for 15 minutes or until golden-brown. Serve warm for dessert, or at room temperature for a snack.

Serves 10

CROISSANTS AUX AMANDES

These are what clever patissiers do with leftovers, recreate them into something even better.

Syrup
⅓ cup water
½ cup sugar
 2 tablespoons kirsch, amaretto, or brandy

 8 leftover croissants, 1 or 2 days old
 1 recipe almond cream (page 175)
⅔ cup sliced blanched almonds
   Confectioners' sugar, for dusting

1. To make the syrup, combine the water and sugar in a small saucepan. Bring to a boil over medium heat, stirring frequently to dissolve all the sugar. Remove from the heat and let cool. Add the kirsch and stir to blend. Set aside.
2. Preheat the oven to 400 degrees F. Split the croissants lengthwise and lay them on a greased baking sheet. With a pastry brush, generously baste both sides of the croissants with the syrup. With a small spatula or knife, spread the almond cream onto the interior sides of the croissants, reserving about one-quarter of the mixture to spread over the tops. Sprinkle about two-thirds of the sliced almonds over the almond cream. Close the croissants. Spread the remaining almond cream over the tops, then sprinkle on the remaining almonds. Dust the croissants with confectioners' sugar.
3. Bake for about 10 minutes, until the almond topping turns deep golden-brown. Let cool slightly on the cookie sheet before serving warm or at room temperature.

Makes 8

ORANGE BLOSSOM FRENCH TOAST

This is they way I like to eat French toast. Eggy challah bread is soaked in a fragrant flowery custard, fried until puffed and golden, then served with more butter, warm honey, and fresh orange slices. It makes a royal breakfast, but I like to eat it for dinner, too.

 6 large eggs
1½ cups milk
 1 tablespoon orange blossom water
 1 tablespoon honey
   Pinch salt
 1 loaf Mrs. Aronson's Orange Juice challah (page 48),
   cut into ¾-inch slices
 4 tablespoons melted unsalted butter, approximately
 3 oranges, peeled, sectioned, white membranes
   discarded
   More honey, warmed, for serving
   More butter, for serving

1. In a large mixing bowl, combine the eggs, milk, orange blossom water, honey, and salt, beating well. Immerse the bread slices in this mixture and let steep for about 5 minutes, or until the slices are soaked through.
2. Place a skillet or griddle over medium-high heat and brush with some of the butter. Place as many bread slices as will fit without crowding in the skillet, and brush the top surface of each slice with more melted butter to seal in the egg. Lower the heat, and cook 7 minutes on each side. When the bread puffs up like a souffle and is golden-brown, it's ready. Don't push it down; serve immediately, with oranges, warmed honey, and more butter.

Serves 6

SAUCES, TOPPINGS, AND OTHER EMBELLISHMENTS

CANDIED GRAPEFRUIT

This is the recipe I've been making for my father for years. Every winter I eat a prodigious amount of grapefruit, saving the peels in a plastic bag in the freezer until I have enough for a batch of candied peels. Freezing the peels before candying them is not only thrifty, but it helps tenderize them as well. If you don't have a bag full of peels when you want to make this recipe, freeze the peels for at least 2 hours before proceeding.

Grapefruit peels
Sugar

1. With scissors, cut however much peel you have into strips about ¼ inch wide. Cover peels with cold water and slowly bring to a simmer in a saucepan. Remove from heat, cover pan and let stand about 1 hour; drain. Repeat this process until peel no longer tastes bitter (about 3 times).
2. Cover peels again with water and boil until they are tender, about 15 minutes. Drain well in colander, pressing out as much water as possible. Pack the peel firmly into a measuring cup and remember how much you have.
3. Return peel to saucepan. For each cup of peel add a cup of sugar. Place the pan over medium heat and cook, stirring, until the sugar has dissolved. Cook peel over medium heat, stirring frequently, until sugar syrup is concentrated. Reduce heat to low and boil the syrup gently. Continue cooking until the grapefruit peel is semitransparent and most of the sugar syrup is boiled away.
4. Drain grapefruit peel in colander. Separate pieces of peel on baking sheets and allow to stand until pieces feel fairly dry. This will take several hours. Sprinkle with enough sugar to give them a crystalline look. Store in air-tight tins or containers, or in sealed plastic bags in the freezer.

OVEN-MADE CARAMEL CORN

2½ quarts freshly popped corn
½ cup (1 stick) unsalted butter
1 cup packed light brown sugar
¼ cup honey
½ teaspoon salt
¼ teaspoon baking soda

1. Spread freshly popped corn on a large, shallow sheet pan. Put it in a very low oven (250 degrees F) to keep warm and crisp.
2. Combine butter, brown sugar, honey, and salt in a 2-quart heavy saucepan. Place over medium heat, stirring, until sugar dissolves. Continue to boil until the mixture reaches the firm ball stage (248 degrees F), about 10 minutes.
3. Remove caramel mixture from heat and stir in baking soda, which will cause it to foam and hiss wildly.
4. Take popped corn from oven and pour hot caramel mixture over it in a fine stream. Stir to mix well. Return to oven until the caramel corn is crisp, about 45 to 60 minutes, stirring every 15 minutes. Cool and then store airtight.

Makes 2½ quarts

LEMON CURD

This is a basic recipe for a lemon curd that is not too thick but holds its shape. It also makes a delightful gift when packed in a pretty jar, tied with a bright ribbon, and presented with a spoon so that your recipient knows that the best way to enjoy lemon curd is straight from the jar.

  5 **large egg yolks**
½ **cup sugar**
   Juice of 4 lemons (about ½ cup)
   Finely grated zest of 2 lemons
  4 **tablespoons (½ stick) unsalted butter, softened**

1. In a medium stainless-steel bowl or in the top of a double boiler (not suspended over any water yet), whisk together the egg yolks and sugar until they are light in color, thick, and hold a 1-second ribbon when the whisk is lifted. Whisk in the lemon juice and zest.
2. Suspend the bowl or double boiler top over simmering water and whisk the curd mixture until it starts to thicken. Add the butter, 1 tablespoon at a time, and continue to whisk until the mixture is thick, about 5 more minutes. It will continue to thicken as it cools. Transfer the curd to a jar or container with a tight-fitting lid and store it in the refrigerator. It will keep for up to 10 days.

Makes about 1 cup

LIME CURD

A sprightly variation on lemon curd (above).

 5 **large egg yolks**
½ **cup sugar**
   Juice of 6 limes (about ½ cup)
   Finely grated zest of 2 limes
 4 **tablespoons (½ stick) unsalted butter, softened**

1. In a medium stainless-steel bowl or in the top of a double boiler (not suspended over any water yet), whisk together the egg yolks and sugar until they are light in color, thick, and hold a 1-second ribbon when the whisk is lifted. Whisk in the lime juice and zest.
2. Suspend the bowl or double boiler top over simmering water and whisk the curd mixture until it starts to thicken. Add the butter, 1 tablespoon at a time, and continue to whisk until the mixture is thick, about 5 more minutes. It will continue to thicken as it cools. Transfer the curd to a jar or container with a tight-fitting lid and store it in the refrigerator. It will keep for up to 10 days.

Makes about 1 cup

CRANBERRY CURD

This is a variation of the lemon curd on page 166, substituting unsweetened cranberry concentrate for the lemon juice. It is a thick, sweet-tart spread with a gorgeous mauve color.

Make sure to use unsweetened cranberry concentrate, available in health food stores, not the frozen sweetened kind available in supermarkets.

 5 **large egg yolks**
½ **cup sugar**
⅓ **cup unsweetened cranberry concentrate**
 3 **tablespoons water**
 4 **tablespoons (½ stick) unsalted butter, softened**

1. In a medium stainless-steel bowl or in the top of a double boiler (not suspended over any water yet), whisk together the egg yolks and sugar until they are light in color, thick, and hold a 1-second ribbon when the whisk is lifted. Whisk in the cranberry concentrate and water.
2. Suspend the bowl or double boiler top over simmering water and whisk the curd mixture until it starts to thicken. Add the butter, 1 tablespoon at a time, and continue to whisk until the mixture is thick, about 5 minutes. The curd will continue to thicken as it cools. Transfer the curd to a jar or container with a tight-fitting lid and store it in the refrigerator. It will keep for up to 10 days.

Makes about 1 cup

KAYA

This recipe is based on one from Sophie Grigson's inspired book, *Gourmet Ingredients,* which she had based upon a thick, sweet Malaysian spread made from coconut milk and flavored with kewra water (an extract made from pandanus leaf). The kewra water (or extract) is available in Indian, Philippine, Malaysian and Indonesian markets, or you can mail order it from Kalustyan. It adds a distinctive, perfumed nuance to the spread, although if you leave it out, the coconut milk steps forward. I like kaya both ways, and I use it exactly as I would lemon curd: in tarts, cakes, over fruit, as a spread for sweet breads, or eaten directly from the jar with a spoon.

  6 **large egg yolks**
  2 **large eggs**
  1 **cup packed light brown sugar**
  ¾ **cup unsweetened coconut milk**
     Juice of ½ lemon
1½ **teaspoons kewra water**
  ½ **cup (1 stick) unsalted butter, softened**

1. In a medium stainless-steel bowl or in the top of a double boiler (not suspended over any water yet), whisk together the egg yolks, whole eggs, and sugar until they are thick and very smooth. Whisk in the coconut milk, lemon juice, and kewra water.
2. Suspend the bowl or double boiler top over simmering water and whisk the kaya mixture until it starts to thicken. Add the butter, 1 tablespoon at a time, and continue to whisk until the mixture is thick, about 5 minutes. The kaya will continue to thicken as it cools. Transfer to a jar or container with a tight-fitting lid and store it in the refrigerator. It will keep for up to 10 days. It also freezes well for up to 3 months.

Makes about 2 cups

RICE PUDDING

This is a very classic, very wonderful stove-top rice pudding recipe. Feel free to play around with the flavorings as they suit your fancies.

3¼ cups whole milk, divided
1 cup heavy cream
⅔ cup sugar
2-inch piece of lemon zest (or use 1 teaspoon grated)
½ teaspoon ground cinnamon
¼ teaspoon ground mace
⅛ teaspoon salt
⅔ cup long-grain rice
2 large egg yolks
2 teaspoons pure vanilla extract

1. Combine 3 cups of the milk, the cream, sugar, lemon zest, cinnamon, mace, and salt in a large, heavy saucepan. Bring the mixture to a simmer. Stir in the rice, cover the pan, and simmer gently over very low heat, stirring occasionally, for 45 minutes.

2. Continue to simmer the pudding gently, stirring occasionally and checking to maintain a gentle simmer, until the rice is very tender and almost all of the milk has been absorbed, about 30 minutes longer. Remove the piece of lemon zest (or leave it in if you grated it).

3. Combine the egg yolks and remaining milk in a small bowl, mixing well. Stir into the pudding and cook very gently, stirring constantly, until the pudding thickens slightly, 2 to 3 minutes longer. Remove pan from the heat and stir in the vanilla.

Serves 4–6

BUTTERSCOTCH PUDDING

Here is an example of nursery food at its most indulgent. This creamy, golden pudding is my favorite "there-there" treat, especially when topped with thinly sliced bananas and bourbon cream (page 178).

 3 cups whole milk
 4 large egg yolks
 ¾ cup packed dark brown sugar
 ¼ cup cornstarch, spooned lightly into a measuring cup (do not pack)
 2 tablespoons cold, unsalted butter, cut into pieces
 2 teaspoons pure vanilla extract

1. In a large, heavy saucepan over medium heat, scald 2½ cups of milk (that is, bring it nearly to a boil, but not quite).
2. Meanwhile, in a mixing bowl, whisk together the remaining ½ cup milk, the egg yolks, brown sugar, and cornstarch until smooth.
3. Pour about 1 cup of the hot milk into the egg yolk mixture and whisk vigorously. Pour the warmed yolk mixture into the pan of hot milk and bring to a simmer, whisking constantly. Simmer the mixture, whisking (be sure to stir at the edges of the pan), for 2 minutes. Remove pan from the heat and whisk in the butter and vanilla. Strain the pudding into a clean bowl. Cover with plastic wrap and chill for 2 to 3 hours.

Serves 4–6

MOCHA CUSTARD FILLING

This mocha custard makes a marvelous filling for Danish, but it is also terrific eaten as a pudding all by itself, or perhaps embellished with unsweetened whipped cream and chocolate shavings.

1¼ cups whole milk
1 cup strong, brewed coffee
⅔ cup sugar
   Pinch salt
3 tablespoons unsweetened cocoa powder
2 tablespoons cornstarch
1 large egg
2 large egg yolks
4 ounces bittersweet chocolate, finely chopped
2 tablespoons unsalted butter
1 teaspoon pure vanilla extract

1. Place the milk, ¼ cup of sugar, and salt in a heavy, medium-size saucepan. Bring to a boil over medium heat.
2. Meanwhile, mix together the remaining sugar, the cocoa, and the cornstarch in a bowl. Whisk in the coffee until smooth and free of lumps. Gradually whisk the hot milk mixture into the coffee mixture; return to the saucepan. Slowly bring mixture to a boil over medium heat, stirring frequently. Simmer gently, stirring constantly, until the mixture is fairly thick, about 2 minutes.
3. In a small bowl, whisk the egg and egg yolks together. Slowly whisk in 1 cup of the hot cocoa mixture. Whisk the egg mixture back into the cocoa mixture in the saucepan. Cook over low heat, whisking constantly, until the mixture becomes slightly thicker, about 3 minutes. Do not allow the mixture to boil. Remove pudding from the heat and stir in the chocolate, butter, and vanilla, stirring to melt the chocolate. Transfer the custard to a clean bowl and lay a sheet of plastic wrap directly on the surface. Chill custard in the refrigerator until cold, at least 2 to 3 hours.

Serves 4–6

CRÈME ANGLAISE

This versatile sauce is nice poured over anything craving a creamy, rich cap, especially ripe fruit.

½ **cup whole milk**
½ **cup heavy cream**
¼ **cup sugar**
 3 **large egg yolks**
 1 **teaspoon pure vanilla extract**
¼ **teaspoon almond extract**

1. Combine milk, cream, and half the sugar in a medium heavy-bottomed saucepan over medium heat. Slowly bring the mixture to boil, stirring to dissolve the sugar; then remove the pan from the heat.
2. Meanwhile, put the remaining sugar, egg yolks, vanilla, and almond extract in a medium bowl and whisk just to blend. While whisking the yolks, gradually drizzle in half the hot cream mixture to temper them. Return the egg yolk-cream mixture to the saucepan and cook over medium heat, stirring constantly, until the custard has thickened slightly and coats the back of the spoon. Remove from the heat and let cool in a large bowl of ice water.
3. Strain the sauce through a fine sieve and refrigerate until ready to serve. The sauce will keep for up to 3 days in the refrigerator.

Makes about 1 cup

PASTRY CREAM

This basic recipe makes a fairly thick, not-too-sweet pastry cream suitable for Danish, fruit tarts, or as a filling for cake.

  2 **cups light cream or half-and-half**
  ¼ **cup sugar**
  2 **tablespoons cornstarch**
  4 **large egg yolks**
     Pinch salt
  ½ **teaspoon pure vanilla extract**

1. In a medium saucepan over medium-high heat, bring the cream and 2 tablespoons of the sugar to a boil. Remove pan from the heat.
2. In a small bowl stir together the rest of the sugar, cornstarch, egg yolks, and salt. Briskly whisk 2 tablespoons of the hot cream mixture into the egg yolk mixture to temper it; then pour egg yolk mixture into the saucepan, whisking well. Return pan to low heat and cook the custard, stirring constantly, until it is thick, about 5 to 7 minutes. Do not let the mixture come to a boil.
3. Remove pan from the heat, stir in the vanilla, and cool the mixture quickly by setting the saucepan in a pan of ice water. Transfer pastry cream to a clean bowl and cover with a sheet of plastic wrap placed directly on the surface to prevent a skin from forming. Chill for at least 2 hours before using. Pastry cream may be refrigerated for four of five days or frozen for three months.

Makes about 1 cup

ALMOND CREAM

If you don't have kirsch or prefer not to use it, substitute ½ teaspoon almond extract.

⅔ cup sugar
10 tablespoons (1¼ sticks) unsalted butter, softened
¾ cup ground almonds
2 large eggs
2 tablespoons kirsch

1. In a food processor or electric mixer, cream the sugar and butter together until the mixture turns smooth and pale. Add the ground almonds and mix until blended. Then beat the eggs in one at a time, mixing until the batter is golden and creamy. Add the kirsch and mix until blended.
2. Store tightly covered in the refrigerator for up to 5 days, or freeze for up to 3 months.

Makes about 2 cups

CARAMEL SAUCE

The sweetness of caramel is cut by citrus in this classic recipe.

1 cup sugar
¼ cup fresh orange juice
½ teaspoon fresh lemon juice
⅓ cup very hot water, or as needed
1 tablespoon unsalted butter

1. In a medium, heavy saucepan, combine the sugar, orange juice, and lemon juice. Stir constantly over medium heat until the sugar dissolves. Continue cooking, stirring occasionally, until the mixture colors to a medium golden-brown, about 8 minutes.

2. Turn off the heat; carefully stir in the hot water and the butter, and continue to stir until the sauce is smooth. If the sauce has hardened, return the pan to low heat and cook, stirring, until the lumps dissolve and the sauce is quite smooth. Serve immediately, or refrigerate in a clean jar and reheat before serving, if desired. It is also good served cold.

Makes about 1 cup

CAJETA

Goat's milk is available in health food store, farmers' markets, and in cans in very large supermarkets. Boiling it down with sugar, as is popularly done in Latin America, creates a thick caramel-type sauce with a slight tang.

2 tablespoons water
½ cup sugar
1 quart goat's milk
Small pinch of baking soda

1. Combine the water and sugar in a large heavy saucepan and bring to a boil over high heat. Cook until the syrup turns golden.
2. Add the goat's milk to the caramel at arm's length; the caramel will sputter and harden but then dissolve as it cooks. Bring to a boil, then reduce the heat slightly and add the baking soda. Cook at a rolling boil, scraping the bottom of the pan with a whisk occasionally to make sure the sauce isn't burning. Cook until thickened and reduced to approximately 1½ cups, about 30 minutes. Strain into a bowl and let cool before refrigerating. Cajeta will keep for two weeks, or three months in the freezer.

Makes about 1½ cups

BOURBON CREAM

You can substitute any other spirit for the bourbon, or leave it out altogether and substitute 2 teaspoons pure vanilla extract. If you use a wire whisk rather than an electric beater (or egg beater), make sure the cream, bowl, and whisk are well chilled. The cream will whip up much faster and thicker that way.

   1 **cup heavy cream**
2 – 4 **tablespoons confectioners' sugar, or to taste**
   2 **tablespoons bourbon**

1. Using a chilled fine wire whisk or an electric mixer, whip the cream until it has thickened. Add the confectioners' sugar and bourbon and whip until soft peaks form.

Makes about 1¾ cups

CHOCOLATE SAUCE

This is one of the easiest, most luscious chocolate sauces I know. It tastes just like a melted chocolate truffle because this sauce is made from the same ingredients. Use the finest bittersweet chocolate you can find, since its flavor will be fairly unmasked in this simple preparation.

2 ounces bittersweet chocolate, finely chopped
½ cup heavy cream
¼ cup rum, kalhua, or coffee

1. Place the chocolate in a small bowl and reserve.
2. In a small saucepan, scald the cream over medium heat (that is, bring it almost, but not quite, to a boil). Pour half of the hot cream over the chocolate and gently stir to melt and blend. Add the rest of the cream and the liqueur or coffee, and stir until smooth.
3. Serve sauce slightly warm or at room temperature. Store for up to two weeks in the refrigerator, or freeze for up to three months. To serve, reheat gently over low heat, or in the microwave, which is great for jobs like this.

Makes 1 about cup

POPPY SEED FILLING

Use this filling for any coffee cake in this book, or make hamantashan, those triangular cookies served at Purim. I do every year, and the poppy seed are always the first flavor to go (although prune is a close second). This recipe makes a lot of filling, but you can freeze any leftovers, or simply halve the ingredients.

Always make sure your poppy seeds are fresh, since they go rancid very quickly. I store mine in the freezer.

½ **pound poppy seeds**
 1 **cup dark raisins**
½ **cup (1 stick) unsalted butter**
½ **cup honey**
 1 **teaspoon grated orange zest**

1. Beforehand, in a medium bowl cover poppy seeds with boiling water and let stand for several hours, or overnight. Drain well.
2. In the bowl of a food processor fitted with a steel blade, process the poppy seeds until they are very finely ground and almost form a paste. Add the raisins and pulse to combine. Add the butter, honey, and orange zest and process until smooth.
3. This keeps well in a sealed jar in the refrigerator for several days and can be frozen for up to three months.

Makes 3 cups

BRANDIED CHERRIES

I keep a jar of these in the fridge supposedly to serve to unexpected guests (which has yet to happen at my house), but mostly to fish out with my fingers and eat in the middle of the night. I have also added them, and a teaspoon or so of their juice, to a glass of champagne for an aperitif.

This recipe is based on one from Rose Levy Beranbaum's indispensable tome, *The Cake Bible*.

 1 jar (2 lb., 1 oz.) water-packed Morello cherries,
    drained (reserve liquid)
 1 cup reserved cherry liquid
 ½ cup sugar
    2-inch piece of lemon peel
 ½ cup kirsch or cognac

1. In a medium saucepan, combine the cherries, cherry liquid, sugar, and lemon peel and simmer, covered, for 1 minute. Remove pan from the heat. Transfer the cherries with a slotted spoon to a pint jar and add the kirsch or cognac.
2. Boil the cherry liquid until it has reduced to ¼ cup, remove the lemon peel, and pour syrup over the cherries. Cover jar tightly and swirl to mix. If planning to store longer than 3 months, add enough liqueur to reach almost to the top of the jar. Cool, cover tightly, and refrigerate.

Makes about 1 quart

RASPBERRY SAUCE

A simple sauce in which the lemon juice perfectly brings out the flavor of raspberry.

¼ **cup water**
¼ **cup sugar**
½ **pint fresh raspberries or 1 cup individually quick-frozen raspberries**
 2 **teaspoons fresh lemon juice**

1. Combine the water, sugar, and raspberries in a small saucepan and bring to a gentle boil over medium heat, stirring a few times to help dissolve the sugar. Remove pan from the heat and stir in the lemon juice.
2. Strain the mixture into a bowl, forcing the raspberry pulp through the sieve but leaving behind the seeds. Let sauce cool, then refrigerate until ready to serve. Store for up to one week in the refrigerator, or three months frozen.

Makes about 1 cup

MAIL ORDER SOURCES

American Spoon Foods, Inc.
(800)-222-5886
P.O. Box 566
Petosky, MI 49770

Dean and Deluca
(800)-227-7714
560 Broadway
New York, NY 10012

Kalustyan's
(212)-685-3451
123 Lexington Avenue
New York, NY 10016

La Cuisine
(800)-328-6722
323 Cameron St.
Alexandria, VA 22314

Williams-Sonoma
(800)-541-1262
P.O. Box 7456
San Francisco, CA 94120-7456

<u>REGIONAL COOKING</u>
<u>FROM</u>
<u>AROUND THE GLOBE</u>

__JAPANESE COOKING FOR THE AMERICAN
TABLE by Susan Fuller Slack 1-55788-237-1/$14.00

__CALIFORNIA FLAVORS
by Mable and Gar Hoffman 1-55788-059-X/$14.95

__GERMAN COOKING
by Marianna Olszewska Heberle 1-55788-251-7/$15.00

__MEXICAN COOKERY
by Barbara Hansen 0-89586-589-0/$14.95

__ORIGINAL THAI COOKBOOK
by Jennifer Brennan 0-399-51099-8/$13.00

__THE PHILIPPINE COOKBOOK
by Reynaldo Alejandro 0-399-51144-X/$13.95

All books available in Trade Paperback